W9-CWT-623

The Picture File

A Manual and a Curriculum-Related Subject Heading List

by
Donna Hill

LINNET BOOKS • 1975

Library of Congress Cataloging in Publication Data

Hill, Donna.
The picture file.

Bibliography: p.
Includes index.
1. Libraries—Special collections—Pictures. 2. Cataloging of pictures. 3. Subject headings. I. Title.
Z692.P5H54 025.3'4'71 74-30360
ISBN 0-208-01472-1

First published 1975 as a Linnet Book,
an imprint of The Shoe String Press, Inc.,
Hamden, Connecticut 06514

Printed in the United States of America

Contents

Preface

This manual and subject heading list for a curriculum-related picture file was developed by the author after seven years as a librarian in the Picture Collection of the New York Public Library, subsequent work on picture files in two colleges in Manhattan, and the last eight years as a librarian at Teachers Central Laboratory, Hunter College Library, where a picture file based upon this scheme is being developed.

Few teaching materials can equal the value for its price of a picture file, since, after a relatively small outlay for equipment and supplies, it can be built from the many beautifully illustrated periodicals and other sources available for the asking. Schools, public libraries, and teachers colleges with budget problems may well consider this means to extend their services at small expense.

However, the usefulness and life of a file of teaching pictures depend entirely upon the care with which the material is chosen and processed and upon how well it is organized. How well the file is organized depends upon its subject headings. A collection based upon an inappropriate list of subject headings or upon headings assigned without any plan becomes more and more difficult to use, invites careless treatment, and may be abandoned soon after the departure of the original collector.

The value of a subject heading list especially designed for a curriculum-related picture file would seem beyond dispute, yet when the author undertook to set up such a file for Hunter College Library no list well suited to that purpose could be found. The best known list for small collections is out of date. Lists developed by large public libraries serving diverse clienteles including commercial artists and designers are too minutely detailed in many categories for a small school collection and are not well related to needs of the curriculum in all areas. The Bibliographic Systems Center of Case Western Reserve University School of Library Science, which houses the Special Libraries Association collection of subject heading lists and classification schemes, reported that no list in their collection covered pictures for the school curriculum. Lists found elsewhere were rudimentary or were intended mainly for pamphlets, which are sometimes combined with pictures in the school library to the disadvantage of both. Individual schools and public libraries may well have made good lists for their own use, but the author did not find any readily available.

When it became apparent that a list would have to be developed for the file at Hunter College Library, a study was made of the structure, terminology, and content of the outstanding picture heading lists accessible, in particular those of the Newark Public Library, as published in *The Picture Collection; Subject Headings* (William J. Dane, 1968), *The Picture File in School, College and Public Libraries* (Norma O. Ireland, revised 1952), and the mimeographed list of the Queens Borough Public Library. These were compared with usage in the Picture Collection of the New York Public Library, whose unpublished checklist of headings became thoroughly familiar to the author while a long-term member of the staff.

From the headings in these four sources a basic list was selected with additions and modifications after a survey was done of school subjects in the curriculum bulletins, elementary and secondary school textbooks, teachers manuals, unit plans, and other materials in the Teachers Central Laboratory, and inquiries were made of teachers and students about the use of pictures in the teaching situation. Subjects related to the curriculum were expanded. With particular needs of the grade school teacher in mind, some new headings related to child development were also devised. These include CONCEPTS, used for pictures which illustrate ideas such as near and far, up and down, big and little, long and short; EMOTIONS for such human feelings as love, fear, and anger; and SKILLS for illustrations of elementary learning such as tying laces, buttoning, zipping, and using simple materials and tools including glue and scissors.

In general, terms chosen were those most likely to be used by teachers and students when asking for pictures, for instance COCOA rather than "cacao." BODY (the human body) was adopted to cover both "anatomy" and "physiology," as well as elementary pictures of body parts, hands, feet, ears, etc. In some cases, however, a comprehensive term was used, such as PETROLEUM rather than gasoline or oil.

"See also" references of particular interest to teachers were added, such as: SEX EDUCATION see also ANIMAL BABIES and FAMILY LIFE. "See also" references were made to be suggestive for the teaching situation rather than comprehensive, and were made in greater detail where need was indicated by classroom demand, such as under the headings HOLIDAYS, SCIENCE, and OCCUPATIONS.

Determining the needs for picture subjects related to the curriculum and choosing terminology were not as difficult as deciding upon an arrangement of the headings that would make the processing and maintenance of a small school picture file expedient and the retrieval of pictures easy.

In some of the subject heading lists studied, an attempt was made to keep like materials together by broad main headings and extensive subheadings, as in one list's use of TRANSPORTATION—SEA—SAILBOATS. A teacher looking for illustrations for a unit on transportation would probably appreciate finding trains, planes, boats, and buses in proximity, but another wanting only a sailboat might find it troublesome to remember, look up, or ask the librarian for that heading. Such lengthy forms would be difficult also for the busy school librarian who had to assign them and supervise the retrieval of pictures.

On the other hand, a strict dictionary arrangement would

make a list impossibly long and would isolate rare items and perhaps cause them to be neglected, as would probably happen if early musical instruments such as "rebabs" and "shengs" were filed individually.

It became apparent that the list would work best if some of the advantages of classifying were incorporated into a dictionary arrangement. Broad headings such as INSECTS, SPORTS, and ANIMALS were adopted where proximity of materials was seen as an advantage and isolation of individual items would be impractical. Other broad headings such as "seasons" were rejected where specific headings such as AUTUMN, etc., proved more expedient. Some broad headings were used with "see also" references to specific headings where coverage was needed both for lesser-known materials and for those frequently called for in the classroom, as in the case of HOLIDAYS see also ARBOR DAY, etc..

Following the practice of the Picture Collection of the New York Public Library, three alphabets are used in this plan, an A–Z file of subjects and separate files for geography and biography.

Further explanation of this plan of subject headings follows in the chapter, "Using the Subject Heading List."

Acknowledgments

The author is grateful to Dr. Eileen G. Cowe and to Dr. Bernice L. Samalonis, both of the Department of Curriculum and Teaching, Hunter College of The City University of New York, for their continuing help and encouragement in the development of the picture file for Teachers Central Laboratory, Hunter College Library, upon which this work was based. Thanks are due to Dr. Mary Field Schwarz, also of the Department of Curriculum and Teaching, Hunter College of The City University of New York, for reviewing the headings for geography, and to Professor Yerchanik Iskenderian, former Head of Technical Services, the Library of The City College of The City University of New York, for many helpful suggestions, particularly for the chapter on using the subject heading list.

The author is grateful also to the staff of the Picture Collection of The New York Public Library for advice about equipment, supplies and procedures, and to the staff of the Picture Collection of the Queens Borough Public Library for suggestions about mounting, housing and filing.

Most essential thanks are due Miss Romana Javitz, former Curator of the Picture Collection of The New York Public Library, for the years of excellent training under her direction which the author had while a member of her staff.

Part One

MANUAL

I. Creating a Picture File

Value and Use of a Picture File

Pictures enliven and enrich the curriculum. They make ideas concrete which may have been vague about objects, places, people, customs, and procedures. They help to develop aesthetic sensitivity and, not least, they give pleasure. The specific uses of pictures in education are infinite and often unforeseen by the collector.

Pictures of whatever kind serve educational purposes—slides, loops, filmstrips, movies, stills or prints—but printed pictures, or flat pictures as they are sometimes called, have a function in education which cannot be made obsolete by any of the technologically advanced visual aids. Unlike films, which require projectors, screens, electrical outlets, darkened rooms, and operators, flat pictures are immediately accessible, making their use much more spontaneous and flexible. They invite a close, personal contact and allow the student to educate himself at his own pace, to remain absorbed for as long as he wishes, or to pass over what he has no need for at the moment. In flat pictures, everything is enticing, nothing is imposed.

Flat pictures, especially if tastefully mounted, can be a source of aesthetic pleasure as objects in themselves, like handsome books, for which there is no counterpart in slides or rolls of film.

When flat pictures are organized by an appropriate subject heading list, with "see" and "see also" references, their potential for educating is enormously increased. Unlike films, the subjects of which are fixed, flat pictures can be selected and combined in endlessly varied sets, to serve innumerable needs.

Having a circulating picture file in the library of a school or teachers college will obviate the need for collections in each classroom and will provide pictures of a scope and technical quality which teachers individually could not hope to equal.

Articles on how to use pictures effectively in the classroom can be found listed in *Education Index*.

Space, Equipment, and Supplies

For an initial outlay of a few hundred dollars, the curriculum-oriented library can build a picture file of professional quality which will have many years of service and beauty. The cost of upkeep and growth of the collection will not be great, since sourccs of free pictures are so many and after the first investment the main expense will be for supplies.

Space. In planning a picture collection, consideration should be given to space as well as to budget. The collection will require files with room for expansion, a work area, a storage place for supplies and for pictures in process, and space for sorting and circulating pictures.

The picture file and the card file of picture subjects should be accessible to borrowers. Table space for borrowers should be nearby. Circulation can be handled along with books at the circulation desk, with a place for storing large envelopes and the necessary charge cards.

The work area should be behind the public scene, since freedom from distraction is desirable and clutter is inevitable. Some shelving will be wanted, preferably at least fourteen inches deep. Space for work tables will be needed near electrical outlets. The work area should have good ventilation and good light.

Equipment. A *dry mounting press*, which costs about two hundred dollars, will prove its worth many times over. This is a simple, heat-controlled machine which bonds pictures to mounts permanently in a few seconds without wrinkles, bulges, buckling, or the mess of glue, paste, or cement, and with results that cannot be matched by any other process for beauty and durability. The technique is so simple that an inexperienced person can mount pictures of professional quality at the first attempt. The cost after the price of the press is about three cents per picture for the dry mounting tissue, plus cost of mounts.

The press comes in several sizes for studio and commercial use, but the practical size for most libraries has a platen of 18½ x 15½ inches, and will mount pictures up to 36 inches wide by any length, in sections. Power consumption of the press is 155 volts A.C., 8.7 amps, 1000 watts. It weighs only about fifty pounds and requires little more space than an office typewriter. The press has a thermostatic control adjustable from 180° to 350°F, with a pilot light indicating when the proper temperature has been reached; it also has a timing flasher.

Besides mounting pictures and photographs, the press will laminate, do cloth backing, and make color or black and white transparencies from clay-coated magazine pages, for use in overhead projectors.

Needed for work with the press is a *tacking iron*, an inexpensive, thermostatically controlled device, for temporarily attaching mounting tissue to pictures and pictures to mounts, holding everything in place until bonded in the press.

Useful also is a *flat weight* which speeds the mounting process and prevents curling of mounted materials. Most useful is the size 20 x 20 inches.

A large *sorting device* is helpful in the alphabetizing and filing of pictures.

A good *paper cutter* is a necessity, and only a good one is worth buying. Care must be taken of the blade, or it will begin to make jagged and inaccurate edges. The most useful size for a picture collection is 18 inches.

A sturdy *work table* is needed for the dry mounting press, the weight and the paper cutter. Helpful also is a drafting table, where tacking and other work can be done.

For the storage of pictures, four-drawer, legal-size *filing cabinets* are recommended, with racks for suspension folders. If the library has funds, *jumbo filing cabinets*, 21 x 21 inches, can be had, which hold pictures up to size 14 x 18 inches, and *chart cases* are available for even larger pictures.

Boxes or *trays* with lids will be needed in the work section for incoming materials such as magazines and for pictures in process. Trays or legal-size wire baskets should be kept in some convenient place, perhaps on top of the files, for loose pictures returned from circulation and new pictures ready to be added to the collection.

Small items of equipment needed are razor blades and a sheath holder, an 18-inch steel-edged ruler for measuring and as a guide in the use of razor blades, a 12-inch clear plastic triangle for making trimming lines and margins, a T-square, and scissors. Editor's shears with long blades which make neat and easy cuts are worth the extra expense. They should be handled with respect and never used for anything but paper.

Library possession stamps will be needed for identifying pictures and the envelopes in which pictures circulate.

Supplies. Dry mounting tissue is the bonding material which holds pictures to mounts; permanent dry mounting tissue is recommended. It comes in various sizes in sheets and rolls, but best for the average picture collection are sheets 11 x 14 inches in boxes of 150.

Other materials which may be wanted are *film* for making transparencies, *laminating film* in either glossy or matte finish for sealing papers under a permanent coating, *dry backing cloth* for hinging or reinforcing maps and charts, and *removable tissue* for temporary mounting or for mounting fragile materials which cannot withstand high temperatures.

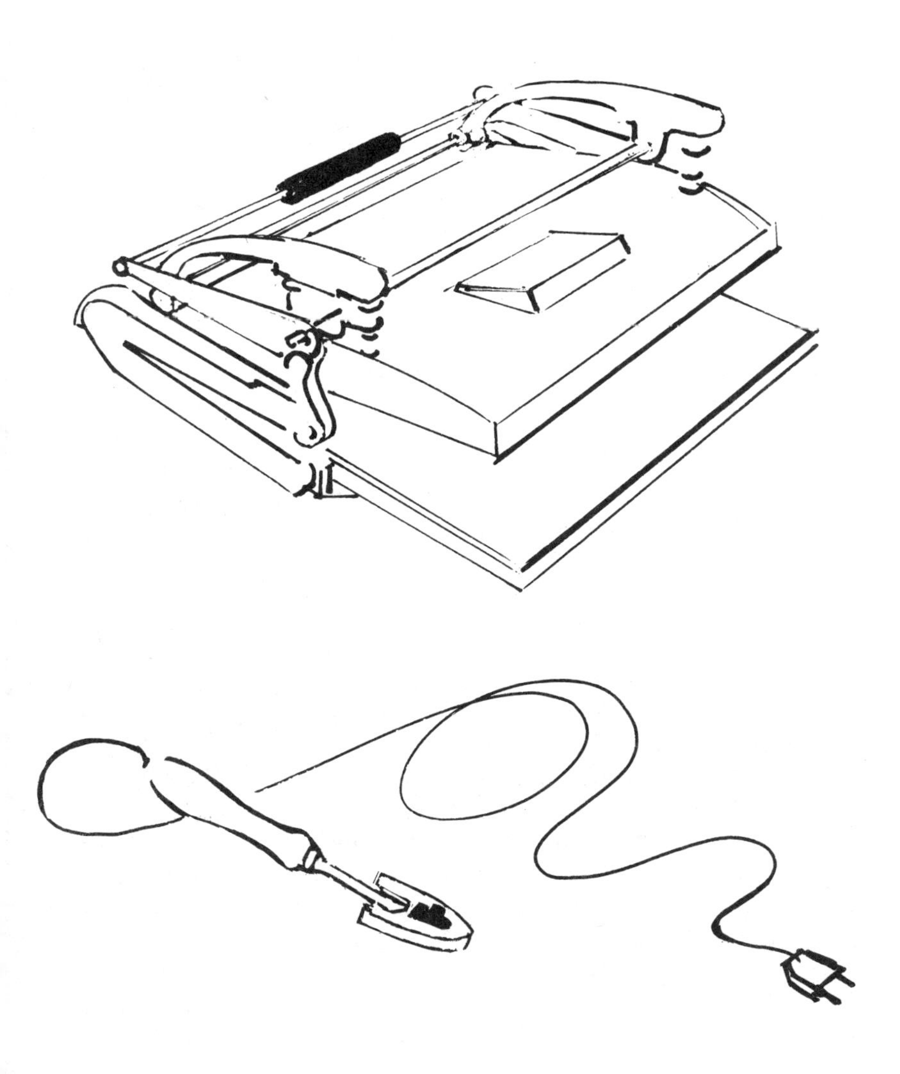

Dry mounting press and tacking iron

It is recommended that all pictures be put on *mounts* of the same size. This will facilitate processing, filing and handling of pictures and will enhance their beauty as a collection. With mounts of the same size, smaller pictures do not get misplaced and larger ones do not get damaged in the files. Using mounts of uniform size presents no difficulty, since it is likely that most pictures will be obtained from books and periodicals with little variation in dimensions. The most expedient size for mounts is 10 x 14 inches or 10 x 14½ inches, which can be accommodated in legal-size filing cabinets.

If the library can afford jumbo filing cabinets or chart cases for even larger pictures, larger mounts will be needed.

It is recomended that mounts be ordered with ⅛-inch holes punched in each corner, about half an inch from the edges, which will allow pictures to be tacked up or hung up on string for exhibiting, without damage to the mounts.

Mounts should be white, of 65-pound weight, and acid free. Lighter stock cannot withstand hard use, while heavier would take up too much space in the files and would have a greater tendency to warp.

Envelopes will be needed in which to lend pictures. Some public libraries have them especially made to withstand very hard use, but these are costly. Most small collections can use the inexpensive red rope expanding envelopes of standard size, 12 x 18 inches, with ribbon closing, usually obtainable from office supply stores.

Miscellaneous items needed include hard pencils No. 3 or No. 4, erasers, rubber fingers, Kraft paper, book pockets, book cards and catalog cards, paper mending tape (as distinguished from transparent tape which should never be used), fixative spray if desired, and self-sticking file folder labels.

Platen cleaner or a substitute such as tuluol or lacquer thinner will be needed from time to time. Platen cleaner is obtainable from the manufacturer of the dry mounting press.

Lists of companies which make or deal in the equipment and supplies needed for a picture collection can be found in such directories as *Educator's Purchasing Guide; Media and Methods* (published by North American Publishing Company, Philadelphia, and revised regularly), and in the

"Purchasing Guide" issues of *Library Journal*, which appear annually, usually in the Spring. The more common items can be found in stationers or in art supply stores.

Sources of Pictures

Periodicals The most fruitful source of pictures for a curriculum-oriented library is usually periodicals. Teachers, students, staff and friends can be asked to donate back numbers of magazines. Doctors, dentists, beauty shop proprietors, and others who have waiting rooms are often willing to give old magazines to a school or library, especially if someone comes to collect them. Although the periodicals should be intact so that the source of pictures will not be lost, age does not diminish their value. Often, old issues are the only practical source of pictures showing changing styles, such as in clothing, furniture, and automobiles. Damaged covers, or dusty and ragged pages may yield good pictures. In the process of mounting, torn or dirty edges will be trimmed and the resulting new vitality to old pages is often surprising. However, magazines with grease spots should be discarded, unless the spots can be entirely cut away, since grease cannot be removed and will spread to other papers in the files.

Subscriptions to a few selected periodicals are well worth the small investment, and if petty cash is available, an occasional trip to a shop selling back numbers can result in many valuable pictures for little expense.

Periodicals of any type with pictures of good quality and size are valuable: women's, men's, and young people's magazines, art, photography, travel, sports, health, and hobby magazines. Good use can be made of popular commercial magazines sold on newsstands or by subscription, such as *Sports Illustrated, American Home, Vogue, Scientific American, Ladies Home Journal, Ebony, Holiday, Fortune, Town and Country,* and *Harper's Bazaar*, and magazines such as *Family Circle*, distributed by supermarkets.

Excellent pictures can often be found in magazines published by special interest organizations issued free to members; some willing to donate back numbers may be among friends of the library. *National Wildlife*, published by the National Wildlife Federation, Inc., is perhaps the best general magazine devoted to preservation of the environment, and has beautiful illustrations of animals, plants, and the outdoors suitable for any class level. *Ranger Rick's Nature Magazine*, published by the National Wildlife Federation for elementary grades, also has excellent pictures of wild animals and other nature subjects. *Sierra Club Bulletin* is known for its many handsome illustrations on outdoor subjects. *Audubon Magazine*, although emphasizing bird life, is devoted as well to the preservation of wildlife in all forms, and has illustrations and color photographs of outstanding quality. *National Geographic* needs no introduction to libraries, where the beauty and value of its pictures have long been well known.

A number of regional magazines such as *Colorado Magazine* and the large and handsome *Maryland Magazine*, devoted to local interests and local history, have numerous superb pictures. *Arizona Highways* has exceptionally beautiful pictures of Southwestern flora, fauna, history, and Indians.

Some international organizations publish magazines of value for the school picture file. *The UNESCO Courier* has good illustrations on such subjects as science, geography, history, art, and music. *Américas*, published by the Organization of American States, has pictures on many aspects of Latin American culture, some of which, expecially the front and back covers, are outstanding.

Magazines put out by commercial organizations for their patrons are also useful. *Mainliner*, by United Airlines, has good illustrations on travel and related subjects. *Travel & Leisure*, published by a subsidiary of American Express for their card holders, and *Signature*, by Diners Club, are similar, with interests extended to sports and fashion.

For their members, some museums publish periodicals

which have pictures of outstanding quality. *The Metropolitan Museum of Art Bulletin* is a superb picture book on art subjects of great variety, based on special exhibitions and on works in the collection, often with an expanded view of the subject not obtainable elsewhere for so little cost; see, for example, their issue on daily life in ancient Egypt.

Smithsonian offers excellent illustrations on archaeology, anthropology, oceanography, natural science, art, and history. Among other museum publications with illustrations of outstanding value for the classroom are *Animal Kingdom*, published by the New York Zoological Society, and *Natural History*, published by the American Museum of Natural History.

Art magazines are of great value to the school and teachers college library. *Art in America*, which usually has about twenty-five full-color plates in each issue in addition to numerous black and white illustrations, is perhaps best as a general source of art pictures; it includes painting, sculpture, architecture, photography, and design.

Graphis, the international journal of applied arts, has notable reproductions of posters, advertising, and related art.

Many other periodicals are devoted to subjects of value to schools, such as *Antiques Magazine, Interiors*, and *American Heritage. African Arts* is richly illustrated, and covers a wide range of cultural aspects of Africa, including art, dance, and sculpture.

House organs are another valuable source of pictures and can often be had for the asking. A useful list of magazines offered free to libraries can be found in *Magazines for Libraries*, by Bill Katz (New York: R. R. Bowker Company). This list describes the periodicals and their illustrations and suggests their value to schools and libraries. More comprehensive lists of house organs can be found in the latest editions of *Gebbie House Magazine Directory* (New Paltz, N.Y.: Gebbie Press) and *The Standard Periodical Directory* (New York: Oxbridge Publishing Company).

Books. Books discarded by staff and friends of the library can be a useful source of pictures. However, pages that are foxed or show other evidence of mould or disease should not be saved, since, as with grease spots, the damage cannot be repaired and will spread to other papers. Again, if petty cash is available, visits to secondhand book stores can be profitable, but more likely are dealers in publishers' overstocks. Remaindered art books at reduced prices may yield many pictures of superb quality, making the cost per print quite small. Many other illustrated books on such subjects as travel, costume, furniture, architecture, Indians, sports, and automobiles, when remaindered, would also be of value to a picture file. Size, quality, and number of prints for the price of the book should be considered in determining the value to the library.

Unless books are rare or expensive, the librarian should feel no reluctance to take out the pictures and discard the text. Books are usually printed in thousands of copies and can be found intact on many library shelves, whereas illustrations removed from one or two copies can be highly useful to teachers and students in a new way when they are made directly available in a file by subject.

Commercial pictures. A number of commercial houses publish sets of educational pictures, but commercial pictures vary greatly in quality. Some are good, but a surprising number are uninspired black and white half tones or poorly rendered drawings, actually inferior to pictures obtainable for nothing. Furthermore, commercial pictures are usually expensive, and some are too fragile for repeated hard use in the school situation. Some commercial reproductions of art intended for student use grossly misrepresent the originals, especially in color. However, some commercial pictures can be useful for subjects difficult to find, for themes needed in sequence, and for portraits. Since it is impossible to determine quality of pictures, especially color and paper stock, from catalogs, it is wise to order one set for examination before buying in quantity.

Free and inexpensive materials. Published lists of free and inexpensive teaching aids are useful if consulted before they go out of date, although when arranged by subject they may require a tedious search for pictures.

An occasional check of *Education Index, Vertical File Index,* and *Bibliographic Index*, under headings such as "free materials" and "teaching aids and devices" will disclose sources of pictures. Some professional periodicals, such as *Today's Education* and *Wilson Library Bulletin*, list free teaching materials.

Many other sources of pictures can be found, such as calendars, posters, book jackets, pamphlets, and annual reports of large corporations. Illustrations from *Book-of-the-Month-Club News* are sometimes useful. Some organizations offer free educational pictures as part of their advertising programs as the National Dairy Council and the American Trucking Associations, Inc., have done. Department stores and dealers in special materials such as educational toys, musical instruments, and sporting goods often publish well-illustrated catalogs.

Many chambers of commerce, airlines, travel agencies, and foreign government tourist bureaus give away pictures, maps, and photographs. Municipal governments sometimes offer publicity photographs of activities in branches such as the sanitation department and port authority. Some state agencies such as the Montana State Highway Commission have put out beautifully illustrated pamphlets. The United Nations offers posters and pictures for a small fee, with price lists available.

Some museums and galleries publish art books and reproductions. The National Gallery of Art puts out a catalog of the educational materials they sell which include excellent and inexpensive art prints and portfolios.

Most publications of the United States Government do not have illustrations suitable for a picture file, although a few departments such as the National Aeronautics and Space Administration publish pamphlets in handsome full color on subjects of their speciality. The National Archives offers photographs of the art work in its collections on such subjects as Indians, American History, the West, and the United States Navy, although the cost per print may make purchase prohibitive for libraries needing pictures in quantity. The *Monthly Catalog* lists these pictures and may sometimes list others.

Many other sources of pictures will occur to the collector

who remains alert. Retiring teachers often have personal collections of prints and scrapbooks they are glad to see put to continued use. The library's own vertical files, book shelves, and periodicals collections may yield valuable pictures when weeded.

Soliciting. For soliciting house organs and other free materials, a form letter should be devised and reproduced on the library or school letterhead. The letter should state the kind of library making the request, and how and by whom the material will be used. Space should be left on the form for the addition of the exact items requested, so that unsuitable material will not be sent. The best response will be had if the date and the company's name and address are individually typed, and the letter is signed personally by the librarian.

Post cards can be sent to organizations offering free materials routinely.

To keep solicited material separate from other incoming mail, the letter or post card should ask that the reply be addressed to the "Picture File," in care of the librarian.

An index of solicited material is well worth the little time it takes and can be done on scrap cards. This file is best kept in two alphabets, pending and received. A third file by subject is also very useful and need not be elaborate.

Files should record date, name and address of the company, and subject of the pictures requested. When material is received, cards from the pending file can be transferred to the permanent file, with a note added of the date and the quality of items. Acknowledgment should be made of all items received in response to a request through the mail. Post card forms can be used but they should be signed by hand.

Unanswered requests should remain in the pending file about a year, since out-of-print items may be reprinted and sent quite a while after they are asked for. Eventually, the card for any material not received should be placed in the permanent file with a note stating why it was not received, if this is known. In the permanent file, these records of material not received can prevent fruitless repeated orders.

Records should be kept only for material solicited through the mail. Items donated voluntarily need not be recorded, and records of items purchased should be kept with book orders.

II. Selecting and Processing Pictures

Selection

As many magazines and other sources of printed pictures should be gathered for a picture collection as can be found, but the final selection of materials to be mounted for the files should be made with great care. It has been said that any picture is better than none. Even though this may be true for an artist's scrap file or for a teacher or a student planning a particular lesson, for a permanent collection of classroom teaching aids, the long range value should be kept in mind. A few good pictures, even one good picture, will serve a useful educational purpose again and again, but poor pictures are not worth the space or cost in supplies and time. The temptation to fill the files as fast as possible should not influence the new collector to lower standards.

Not everyone who wants to start a picture file is an expert in visual arts, or need be, at first. A few simple criteria for selecting pictures will help an inexperienced person build a good collection, while gaining the knowledge of pictures that comes only with a long period of handling, studying, and comparing them.

Pictures in the curriculum-oriented library must represent the subject, or at least the main details, vividly and clearly, and if possible should have some impact from a little distance.

If rendered, the pictures should be skillful in technique, accurately drawn, pleasing in color, and of good design. An appreciation of skill in design, technique, and perhaps color may have to be acquired gradually by the new collector, but most people can recognize poor drawing, contrived, sentimental or "cute" pictures, and should learn to resist them. If there is reason to begin the visual arts training of children with simplified pictures, this does not mean inferior pictures.

Pictures should be as large as the filing space will permit, after mounting. Printing has become so sophisticated that many beautiful pictures can be found of post card or even postage stamp size, but for a teaching file, the value of mounting pictures which are smaller than about 6 x 8 inches, depending somewhat upon carrying power, is questionable.

Picture post cards are often useful to teachers, especially with an opaque projector. They should be chosen with care for their educational value and given the same headings as pictures, but they are best kept unmounted in a separate file.

Pictures should be in color rather than black and white, whenever possible, exceptions of course being art reproductions such as drawings and etchings in which color is not a factor, and subjects not likely to be found in color, such as some portraits and art photography. Beautiful color printing is now so universal that black and white half tones or sepia need not often appear in the collection.

Quality of paper is to some extent a consideration in building a lasting picture file, but with techniques of dry mounting, pictures on paper which might formerly have been thought too poor, fragile, or worn to preserve, such as newsprint or pages from brittle old books, can be made quite substantial and worth collecting, as long as other qualities make them of value.

Advertisements should be used only if brand names and text can be trimmed away completely, leaving a square or rectangular picture. Advertisements obviously posed or contrived should in general be avoided, except perhaps for fashions.

Since it is difficult to imagine any subject not useful in a picture file, discrimination on the basis of content is necessary only to avoid too large a file of certain popular subjects such as Christmas and flowers.

For a picture of some item which is rare but likely to be useful, such as a howdaw or an arbalest, it may be necessary to make adequate size and clarity of printing the only consideration.

No original work should ever be kept in the files with printed materials, since it would be a disservice to both.

Criteria for selection of pictures can most readily be applied by a beginning collector when a great many pictures are available from which to choose. At the outset, it is recommended that only pictures of unquestionable merit be mounted for the collection, but that a large preliminary selection of pictures be made and held for further consideration.

In building a curriculum-oriented file, the librarian should be watchful to acquire representation of all races in the society, especially in scenes of family, school, professional, and community life, and in children's play and holiday activities. Pictures of various religious and ethnic groups should also be obtained, and of the sexes in roles besides those which custom has decreed. With pictures of women as politicians, police officers and jockeys, men in unconventional roles as well, and members of the minorities in the professions, the arts and all activities of the community, the richness and variety of contemporary life may be brought into the classroom and vistas kept wide for all children.

Storing Pictures in Process

Books to be cut up for pictures can be kept on shelves, but periodicals, which are more fragile and need better protection from dust and accidents, should be stored in a large box with a lid. Several other boxes or trays with lids will be needed for loose pictures in various stages of processing and for mounted pictures until they can be stamped, classified, and added to the files.

Since loose pictures are often held for weeks or months, especially those given only a preliminary trimming or tacking, they should be stored carefully. It is best to "corner" them, that is, to fit them alternately and neatly into each of the four corners of the box in turn, so that a flat, even pile is built regardless of the dimensions of the pictures. This keeps the paper from crumpling and curling, preserves edges, and allows more pictures to be stored than would be possible if they were thrown into the box haphazardly.

Recording Identity of Pictures

It is important for a library which serves artists, writers, editors, and others who may need copyright data and other bibliographic information for publication to record carefully the source of pictures. The school or teachers college library may not often serve such a need, but users of the file may want to know where the pictures came from so that they can consult the text. While loss of the source may be sufficient reason to discard a picture from a public library, in a school collection a good picture without source can have a useful life. Loss of the identification of the subject, however, such as name of artist, place, person, or species, usually means the value of the picture for educational purposes is destroyed. This of course does not apply to pictures of general subjects such as winter, children at play, or Valentine's Day.

Books. When a great many books will be cut up for pictures, the work of indicating source can be eased by assigning an accession number to each book and recording the bibliographic information by that number in a card file, as is done by the Picture Collection of the New York Public Library. For easy reference, the accession number is written in the same place in the center of the lower margin of each picture from the book. If few books will be used for the school picture file, the librarian may consider it easier to enter the author, title, and date of the book on each picture itself.

All relevant information about the subject, such as name, place, date, size, material, medium, artist, style, country, classification, or origin, should be recorded under the accession number of each picture. After each picture is identified, the cover of the book should be removed by cutting the gutters with a razor blade in a sheath holder or a very sharp knife. Pictures can then be torn free from the binding and the text discarded.

Periodicals. In working with periodicals, the staples should first be removed and the cover saved for reference. The magazine should be gone through quickly page by page and the whole page on which any picture is wanted torn from the spine. Before the cover and text are discarded, the name and date of the publication and any other pertinent information should be recorded on each picture, preferably in the center of the bottom margin, but in any event never on the back, where it may inadvertently be lost when the picture is mounted.

For pictures having no margins or useable light space, the information can be kept separately. In this instance, some means of identifying the picture must be used, a number assigned, or a description noted, so that data can be matched later with the proper picture and added to the mount.

Any information added to pictures or mounts should be written in hard pencil, No. 3 or 4.

Mounting

Most pictures chosen for the file should be mounted to insure longer life under hard use in the teaching situation and for better appearance. However, some pictures on heavy stock, as large or nearly as large as the mounts, and perhaps with valuable text on the back, may be added to the collection without mounting, but should be given the library accession stamp and classified in the usual way. If the unmounted pictures are somewhat smaller or more flexible than the mounting boards, they can be kept in manila folders, preferably the kind closed on three sides, and filed directly in front of mounted pictures of the same heading. The manila folders as well as the pictures kept in them should be labeled. Suspension folders holding mounted pictures need not be labeled, since the pictures stand above the folders in the file and index themselves.

For best service, put the dry mounting press on a sturdy table or bench at good working height. With the press closed, the handle will be to the front. To open the press, lift the handle and push it to the back. It must be pushed all the way back to prevent accidental closing.

The new press will have a piece of quarter-inch masonite on the bed of the press. Remove this, since it is to be used only in laminating. The bed is covered with a sponge rubber pad which compensates for variation in thickness between picture and mount, allowing uniform pressure over the whole surface.

Plug the press into a three-way outlet of standard 115 volts, A.C. . If an extension cord is used with the press, it must be made for heavy duty.

For most work, set the thermostat at 225°F and preheat the press. A cold press will require about eleven minutes to reach 225°F.

Since all paper absorbs some moisture from the air, it is advisable, especially in humid weather, to preheat the picture and mount before bonding, to dry and flatten them and prevent warping. Place print and mount in the heated press and pull the handle forward only until the top rests lightly on the material. Usually pictures will dry within ten seconds, but in very humid weather from one to five minutes may be necessary. During longer periods of drying, open the press for a moment or two every 45 to 60 seconds.

Set the temperature control on the tacking iron at "hi" and preheat. The tacking iron can be plugged into any convenient outlet or extension cord and will heat much faster than the press.

To avoid waste of mounting tissue, trim all unnecessary borders, text and advertising from the picture before it is tacked. If any of the picture itself is trimmed, write "detail" on the picture or mount, with the other information about it. In trimming, take care not to lose any of the identification.

It is usually best to discard pictures which cannot be trimmed to a rectangle or square, as when irrelevant text or brand names intrude into the picture space. An excellent picture of a rare subject which has unwanted print running into the picture space may be cut out in outline and mounted, but this is not usually worth the time it requires.

Cut a piece of dry mounting tissue slightly larger than the picture, allowing about an eighth of an inch overlap on each side of the picture. Place the picture face down on a clean surface with the tissue over it (tissue has the same heat sensitive adhesive on both sides). With the tip of the warm tacking iron press one or two strokes in the center of the tissue to attach it to the picture. Leave the corners free to allow for expansion in the press and to prevent wrinkles and bubbles.

For economy, save the larger scraps of mounting tissue. They can be used by overlapping the patches slightly and tacking each patch to the back of the picture, which can then be trimmed and mounted as usual.

Trim the picture and the tissue together on the paper cutter, keeping perfect right angles at all corners. To remove a very small slice of mounting tissue, use a razor blade (in a holder) with the steel-edged ruler.

Lay out the picture on the mount so that the margins are even on the sides, widest at the bottom and narrowest at the

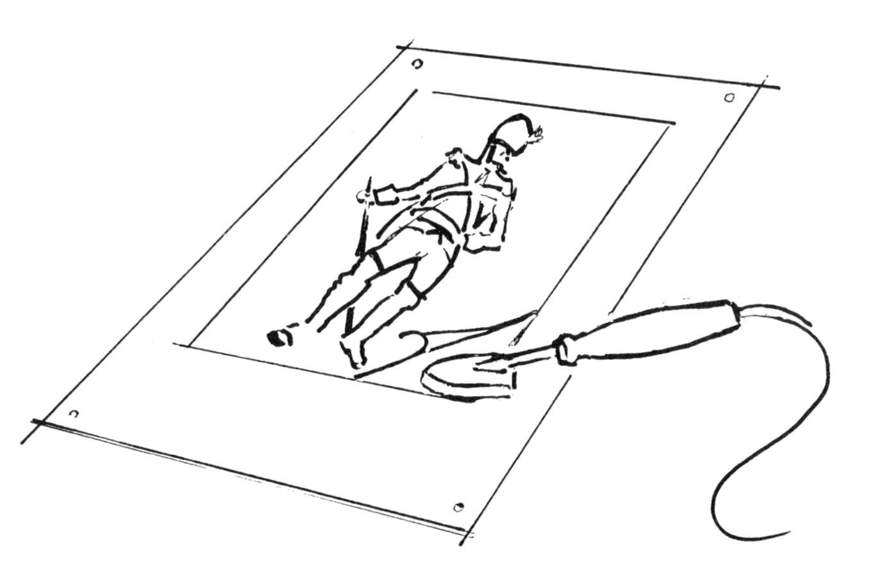

Lift two corners of the picture and tack the tissue to the mount in two spots.

top. With mounts of uniform dimensions and pictures of various sizes and shapes, it is not always possible to achieve this ideal, but the sides should be even and the bottom margin wider than the top.

Holding the picture and tissue in place on the mount, lift two corners of the picture and tack the tissue to the mount in two spots. This will prevent the picture from slipping out of place before it has adhered.

Place the picture and mount in a fold of any clean, porous paper, such as Kraft, and put in the heated press. Close the press and lock it by pulling the handle down completely. The timing device, a red light on top of the press, will go on and in a second or two will begin to flash. If there is fluctuation of voltage in the electric line into which the press is plugged, the flashes may vary slightly, but this will not affect the work.

The average picture will adhere to its mount in from twelve to twenty flashes, but there is little danger if the picture is left in the press somewhat longer, since the dry mounting tissue has been made to accommodate temperatures from 200°F to 275°F for from five to about forty seconds. Photographs and heavy papers need more time and some papers a hotter press than average. If after removal from the press, the picture pulls away from the mount, or if bubbles appear, the picture should be returned to the press for a few more seconds. After a little experience, the operator will be able to judge the time and temperature needed for various materials.

Pictures can also be mounted with dry mounting tissue and an ordinary household iron, the control set at *silk*. Use the tip of the iron for tacking. Bond picture to mount with a slow, circular motion.

Place the warm picture under a weight for a few minutes. Good for this purpose is the flat metal weight size 20 x 20 inches sold by the manufacturer of the dry mounting press. This is designed to speed the mounting process by drawing heat from the material and eliminating any tendency to curl.

Some protection from smudges can be given to pictures and mounts by fixative spray, if desired, but laminating or covering pictures with plastic has not proved worth the added cost and labor for a whole collection.

Labels. Although subject headings can be written on picture mounts directly, the use of labels adds to the life and appearance of a collection and allows easy change without damage to mounts. Self-sticking white labels are the most expedient.

On horizontal pictures, labels should be attached to the upper *left* corner, about one quarter of an inch from top and side, on the front of the mount or on the picture itself if it is not to be mounted. On vertical pictures, the label should be attached to the upper *right* corner, along the length of the right margin. This will bring the top of all vertical pictures to the left when put in the files, so that headings for all pictures horizontal and vertical will be in the same position. Care in positioning labels eliminates the awkward need to turn the head when filing or searching. Since headings may be changed frequently, they should be printed in plain block letters in hard pencil, No. 3 or 4.

Possession Stamps. Pictures in a library or school collection should receive a possession stamp. In large public libraries where it is necessary to identify both mount and picture, a stamp of about two and a half inches is used on the back of mounts, and on the lower right corner of the picture, a stamp no longer than one inch is used so as to deface the image as little as possible. In collections where risk of pilferage is slight, stamping the back of the mount may be sufficient.

III. Circulation and Maintenance of the Collection

Circulation

There is no better stimulus to the use of a picture file than the opportunity to look through it and enjoy it freely. For this reason, and because subject headings, no matter how thoughtfully assigned, can never bring out every useful aspect of a picture, the files should be open and made convenient for browsing, with table space nearby where users can take folders to examine at their leisure.

Pictures should probably circulate for as long as books, and charging procedures can be similar, except that an envelope should be provided and the borrower as well as the library should have a record of the number and subjects of pictures and of the date due. It is convenient to use a call slip which makes a carbon for filing, so that the original can be put in a book pocket attached to the envelope. Some libraries write the information directly on the envelope.

It is advisable to limit the number of pictures borrowed at one time. At the outset the number should be small, perhaps ten, which can be increased according to need after the collection has grown. Pictures should be brought to the circulation desk and counted by both the borrower and the library assistant. The pictures should be counted again and examined for condition when returned.

The envelope in which pictures are lent should have a

library possession stamp. On the envelope, perhaps on the book pocket, it should be stated that pictures must be returned in complete sets as borrowed and that a fee is charged for the loss of pictures or for damage to pictures or mounts. It is expedient also to add in bold letters: DO NOT MARK, STAPLE, GLUE, FOLD, or TAPE.

Since a picture lost or damaged beyond use can seldom be exactly replaced, fines will not be truly representative of value, but should impress responsibility for the pictures upon the borrower. The amount should be set by the librarian before any pictures begin to circulate, and should take into account the cost of labor and supplies.

Care of Pictures

The filing system which makes use of suspended folders will add years of life to the picture file as well as a great deal of ease and speed in filing and maintaining order in the collection. Suspended folders, and the tracks installed for them in the files, are somewhat more expensive at the outset but not in the long run, because they have a much longer life than conventional folders. Filing and searching are greatly simplified because all subject headings remain on the same level, and folders whether thick or thin remain in place, with none sliding to the bottom of the file. Mounts and pictures are thus protected from curling and damage to corners.

In contrast to a pamphlet file, a picture file, if materials are well chosen from the outset, will never need a systematic weeding. Pictures should be discarded only if they become damaged beyond repair. Grease and oil spots, for instance, are very destructive to paper and will spread to whatever papers lie adjacent. Unless the spots can be trimmed away entirely and the picture remounted, the picture should be discarded.

Pencil marks should be removed with a gum or kneaded

eraser, but a little spattering of glue, ink, or water-base paint can be tolerated if not so defacing that the value of the picture is lost.

Tears can be mended with paper mending tape, but transparent tape should never be used, since eventually it will ooze and spread a destructive yellowish substance. Staples and paper clips are also destructive to paper and should never be used on pictures.

A picture on a damaged mount can best be salvaged by trimming the edges of the mount and remounting under a slightly higher temperature and longer period, to allow the heat to penetrate the double thickness of mounting board. The result will be a heavier picture, but still useful.

Pictures which have been mounted by paste or glue can usually be taken off their old mounts, preferably by tearing the mount bit by bit from the picture, rather than by trying to skin or pull the picture off the mount. Pictures which have been dry mounted are in permanent bond with the mount, and attempts to separate them most often result in destruction of the picture, unless the mount itself can be split and part of it left with the tissue on the back of the picture. This, however, is difficult and hazardous. If desired, a mounting tissue is available which does not form a permanent bond.

Care of the Dry Mounting Press

Oilite bushings are used in the pivot positions of the press, but other moveable parts will occasionally need a few drops of oil.

To remove deposits of adhesive from the platen, tuluol or a lacquer thinner may be used, or platen cleaner obtained from the press manufacturer. The press should be heated to 225° F to soften the deposits and then unplugged before cleaning, since solvents are flammable. Stubborn deposits may be removed by a fine grade of emery cloth or a razor blade, but care should be taken to avoid scarring the platen.

The machine should be covered when not in use.

Training Assistants

Library assistants should be trained to do the routine work in building and maintaining the collection, such as soliciting materials and keeping records, preliminary selection of pictures, simple sourcing and identifying (which should be reviewed by the librarian in charge), accessioning, circulation, and filing. Decision as to what materials to solicit, the final selection of pictures to be mounted, assigning subject headings, and all but the simplest identifying should be done by the librarian, who should also keep the statistics.

Mounting and processing should be done by assistants. Care should be taken in teaching each step in mounting, so that good, safe habits are established and work of high quality produced. Prudent use of the tacking iron, the dry mounting press, and the paper cutter should be emphasized, since they can be dangerous if mishandled.

Particular care should be taken from the start in teaching the assistants how to position the picture on the mount for a regular and pleasing relationship of picture to margins, which more than any other factor, besides the flat bonding, gives the work a professional appearance.

IV. Using the Subject Heading List

A librarian who is planning to organize a picture file based upon the following subject heading list should read through the list and should master its underlying principles as set forth here. A thorough understanding of the list is essential for the proper assignment of headings and for the upkeep and development of the collection. It will remain necessary for the librarian to assign headings with the list at hand and to refer to it constantly.

A picture collection based upon this plan will have three sections: (1) subjects A-Z; (2) geography, which includes inhabitants who are not distinguished as individuals and history since the rise of modern nations; and (3) biography, which includes related materials. This manual provides headings for the subjects A-Z file and the geography file and instructions for setting up the biography file.

This printed list of headings, or checklist as it may hereafter be called, is the librarian's working tool for establishing and building the collection. The librarian should build a card catalog of picture subject headings and cross references based upon this checklist for the use of those who borrow pictures. Instructions on using the checklist and on building the card catalog follow.

The Checklist. *Subjects A-Z.*

Headings to be assigned to pictures, arranged in alphabetical order, will always appear in *capital letters.*

Under each heading additional information, if any, will always be given in the following sequence:

(1) a scope note defining the heading or telling what it is intended to cover
(2) instructions on how to make subheadings in addition to the ones specifically given
(3) "see also" references
(4) tracings from "see" references
(5) tracings from "see also" references
(6) subheadings to be added from the outset of the collection
(7) tracings from "see" and "see also" references to subheadings
(8) headings in phrases

The following example shows each of the above elements except a scope note, which was not needed in this case, and headings in phrases.

FLOWERS AND PLANTS
(subdivided further by name of flower or plant)
see also GRAINS AND GRASSES
MOSS
TREES
x plants
xx BOTANY
——STATE
x state flowers

An explanation of these elements follows, in the order in which they appear in the example.

Subheadings. Directions, if any, on how to make subheadings are given immediately after the heading. In the above example, the heading to be written on a picture of a rose would be FLOWERS AND PLANTS. (The information that the flower is a rose should be added to the bottom of the picture or mount.) When enough pictures of roses have been collected to make a separation in the files worth while, the subheading ROSES should be added, so that headings on all pictures of roses will read: FLOWERS AND PLANTS—ROSES.

The reason subheadings are not added before a number of pictures of that subject have been collected is to keep filing as simple as possible, so that alphabetizing by each individual item will not be necessary.

In some cases, geographic subheadings are indicated, as in the following:

AIR FORCE
(subdivided further by adjective of country)

This indicates that the adjective form of a country's name is used, for instance, when enough pictures of the French Air Force have been added to make a separation from the main file expedient, the heading AIR FORCE—FRENCH would be added. The word FRENCH and not France is used; GERMAN not Germany, etc. To this there are two exceptions: UNITED STATES is used because there is no satisfactory adjective form of that word and because AMERICAN, where used, includes both continents. The heading MAPS takes the subheading in the noun form because it would not make good sense otherwise, i.e., the heading would be MAPS—FRANCE.

See below for an explanation of subheadings which should be used from the outset of a collection, without waiting for a number of pictures to collect.

"See also" references. "See also" references give directions to other headings that may be used for related or more specific subjects. The example above indicates that other related headings which may be used where appropriate are GRAINS AND GRASSES, MOSS and TREES. The *most*

specific heading which appears in the list in all capital letters should be selected for use on each picture. Sometimes a dictionary, encyclopedia, or other source will be needed to establish proper identity of the subject, for instance whether it is a grass or a tree.

"See also" references are made: (1) to related terms, or (2) to more specific terms. They are not made from specific terms to more general terms.

"See" references and tracings from "see" references. In this list will be found some words or groups of words in lower case. These are "see" references, or directions from a word or group of words which is *not* to be used on pictures to headings which should be used. Such words or groups of words are included in the list to prevent the scattering of like materials throughout the file under more than one heading. Occasionally the "see" reference will be from the second part of a compound heading to the whole heading, as in the following:

plants see FLOWERS AND PLANTS

A record of the "see" references is made under the heading to which it refers. It is called a "tracing" and is preceded by "x". Where two or more tracings occur, they are listed alphabetically, but only the first will be preceded by "x", as in the example:

POSTAL SERVICE
x mailmen
pony express

This example gives the information that in the list in alphabetical order will appear the following:

mailmen see POSTAL SERVICE
pony express see POSTAL SERVICE

Tracings not only tell the user of the checklist what "see"

references appear in the list for that heading, but help to indicate what the heading should cover. In the above instance, the librarian will know that pictures of mailmen and pony express riders will be given the heading POSTAL SERVICE.

If headings in the list are ever changed or removed, the tracings will indicate which references must be changed or removed as well, so that no dead ends remain.

Unlike the usual practice in libraries, "see" references in this list may refer to more than one heading.

Tracings from "see also" references. Where "see also" references exist for a heading, a record of those references will appear under the heading. These too are called tracings, but they will appear in all capital letters, since they may be used as headings, and they are preceded by "xx." Tracings for "see also" references follow tracings for "see" references, as in the example under FLOWERS AND PLANTS above.

Where there are two or more tracings from "see also" references, they are listed alphabetically, but only the first will be preceded by "xx," as in the following example:

POLLUTION
x air pollution
environment
xx CONSERVATION
ECOLOGY

This example indicates that "air pollution" and "environment", which are *not* to be used as headings, will have "see" references in the list. CONSERVATION and ECOLOGY, which may be used as headings where appropriate, will have "see also" references in the list.

Subheadings which should be used from the outset of a collection.

The last item in the example given above under FLOWERS AND PLANTS is a subheading which should be applied to pictures from the outset of a collection, without waiting for the collection to grow.

In the checklist, subheadings are preceded by a dash to eliminate repetitions of the main heading, but the full heading must always be written out on pictures. From the above example, the heading for a picture of any state flower would be FLOWERS AND PLANTS—STATE. Identification of the individual state flower would be given at the bottom of the picture or mount.

Subheadings may also have tracings. In the example above, the tracing indicates that in the list the following will appear:

state flowers see FLOWERS AND PLANTS—STATE

The Checklist: Geography File

Headings in the geography checklist are based upon usage in *Webster's New Geographical Dictionary*, G & C Merriam Co., 1972, although some substitutions have been made for names in more popular use in the classroom such as SOUTH SEA ISLANDS for Oceania. The list is not intended to be comprehensive, but rather to include countries most likely to receive attention in the school curriculum. Since names and political divisions frequently change, as do needs of the curriculum, the librarian should be alert to keep the list current. However, rather than changing headings with each new name or political unit, it is advisable as a rule to retain original headings and make cross references to them from the new names.

The headings are intended automatically to cover history since the rise of modern nations, although where many pictures are likely to be collected, a separate subheading for history is suggested for use at the outset.

Pictures of people in native dress or otherwise representative of countries are placed in the geography file, except for the following, which are to be in the subject file: American

Indians of both continents; Eskimos; Gypsies; people illustrating a concept or an activity such as SPORTS or FAMILY LIFE; people in historical subjects such as BLACK HISTORY—UNITED STATES; EXPLORATIONS; and MIDDLE AGES; and people in countries previous to the rise of modern nations, such as EGYPT—ANCIENT; GREECE—ANCIENT; and ROME—ANCIENT. Portraits of explorers, such as Columbus, belong in the biography file, but renderings of Columbus in action are filed with EXPLORATIONS.

Countries are in the geography file directly under their own names, with the exception of South African and Caribbean countries; it has been found expedient to keep these countries in proximity.

The headings for continents, ASIA, etc., are for subjects which can belong to more than one country in the continent, such as rivers, mountains, or sometimes people.

To this list it is recommended that the librarian add a heading directly under its own name for the city in which the library is situated, such as CHICAGO or TUSCON, with a cross reference under UNITED STATES—STATES.

The letter "G" should precede headings assigned to pictures for the geography section, as an aid in filing.

The Checklist: Biography File

The biography file is intended to include not only portraits but any pictorial material related to the individual, for instance pictures of monuments to him, his home, pets, studio, family (with cross references to any family members of interest in their own right). However, works by the biographee, such as architecture or paintings, go in the subject file.

A checklist for a portrait file is not feasible. However, where more than one name is found for the same person, such as a pen name, or when more than one spelling is possi-

B. Chaikovski, Pëtr Ilich

see

B. TCHAIKOVSKY, PETR ILICH

B. TCHAIKOVSKY, PETR ILICH

x B. Chaikovsky, Pëtr Ilich

Biography cards

Top: "See" reference
Bottom: Name chosen for use in the catalog with tracing from form of name not used

ble, a card file should be kept to record the name chosen for use by the library.

Choice of name should follow the practice established for the library's book collection, but if the name is not in the catalog, some standard reference tool should be consulted. Failing that, as with perhaps a locally known person, popular usage may be accepted.

"See" references should be made from all variants to the name chosen.

More important than the choice or spelling of a name is that all portraits of an individual be kept together.

The letter "B" should precede headings assigned to pictures for the biography section, as an aid in filing.

The Card Catalog

The checklist is the librarian's working tool for establishing and developing the picture collection. For the use of teachers, students and others who borrow pictures, the librarian should build a card catalog of headings, "see" and "see also" references based upon the checklist but representing only pictures which are actually in the file.

A complete set of cards should be made for each new subject added to the picture file. A check mark in pencil should be made beside the heading in the checklist as soon as the cards are made, to enable the librarian to tell at a glance which subjects are represented in the collection.

Cards in the picture file catalog should follow the style of the checklist, with headings in capital letters and cross references in lower case. Sample cards should be kept for each kind of entry, so that style and spacing will be consistent throughout the card catalog.

Scope notes, "see" and "see also" references as shown in the subject heading list will be helpful in the picture files, on cards of folder size. However, they do not replace the card catalog of picture subject headings.

```
        FLOWERS AND PLANTS





 x plants
xx BOTANY
```

```
        FLOWERS AND PLANTS

           see also

        GRAINS AND GRASSES

        MOSS

        TREES
```

Subject cards

Top: Heading with tracings from "see" reference and "see also" reference
Bottom: Heading with "see also" references.
This card would follow the above in the catalog

```
        MOSS




xx FLOWERS AND PLANTS
```

```
            plants

            see

        FLOWERS AND PLANTS
```

Subject cards

Top: Heading with tracing from "see also" reference
Bottom: "See" reference

```
        G.  Arab Republic

        see

     G.  EGYPT
            (modern)
```

```
     G.  EGYPT
            (modern)




x G.  Arab Republic
```

Geography cards

Top: "See" reference
Bottom: Heading with tracing from "see" reference

Expanding the Subject Heading List

Headings and subheadings can be added to this list to answer growing needs, but care must be taken to preserve the integrity of the list. The basic concepts of the list should be kept in mind, which are that subjects should reflect the needs of the school curriculum and that terms chosen are those in common use by teachers and students, and are most likely to be used by them in making requests for pictures. Occasional exceptions may be made where a more comprehensive term would allow for better coverage of the material, as has been noted in the case of PETROLEUM, used to cover gasoline and oil.

In each case, before a new heading is added, the checklist should be read through, to make sure that the proposed idea is not already covered by another term, which would make only a "see" reference necessary. A dictionary or other reference work should be consulted before final decision about the term is made, to ensure that it is exact and unambiguous.

Assigning Headings

Much of the pleasure in building a picture file is in assigning subject headings to pictures. This should be seen as a challenge to the imagination. It is necessary to consider what purpose each picture can best serve and in some cases how many pictures are already in the file under the heading contemplated. It is important also to think about how well the picture may illustrate alternative subjects, and whether or not it could be used in a category where there are as yet few or no pictures.

The most obvious subject of a picture may not be the only or even the best or most interesting place for it. A reproduction of an Egyptian mural, for instance, could be used not only under ART or EGYPT—ANCIENT, but, depending on content, under any of a number of other headings, such as COSTUME, IRRIGATION, DANCE, MUSIC, FAMILY LIFE, FUNERALS, or FARMING. An imaginative application of subject headings will help stimulate teachers and students who use the file to an imaginative approach to the curriculum.

Part Two

SUBJECT HEADING LIST

I. Subjects A-Z

Note: Only words or phrases in *capital letters* should be used as headings on pictures. Words or phrases in lower case are "see" references only, or, when preceded by "x", are tracings from "see" references. See explanation in preceding chapter.

abacuses see MATHEMATICS
ABBEYS
see also CONVENTS
MONASTERIES
xx ARCHITECTURE
Abraham Lincoln's Birthday see LINCOLN'S BIRTHDAY
ACCIDENTS
acoustics see SOUND
acrobats see CIRCUS
action see MOVEMENT
adolescents see YOUTH
ADVERTISING
see also POSTERS
x trade-marks
xx SIGNS AND SYMBOLS
AERONAUTICS
see also AIRPLANES
SPACE FLIGHT

AERONAUTICS (continued)
x airports
balloons
dirigibles
flight
helicopters
parachutes
xx TRANSPORTATION
——HISTORY
Afro-Americans see BLACK HISTORY
agriculture see FARMING
AIR FORCE
(subdivided further by adjective of country)
——UNITED STATES
air pollution see POLLUTION
AIRPLANES
x planes
xx AERONAUTICS
TRANSPORTATION
——HISTORY
airports see AERONAUTICS
alligators see REPTILES
alphabets see LETTERS
WRITING—HISTORY
AMPHIBIANS
x frogs
toads
AMUSEMENT PARKS
x merry-go-rounds
AMUSEMENTS AND GAMES
see also SPORTS
x games
anatomy see BODY
ANCHORS

ancient history see HISTORY—ANCIENT
ANGELS
ANIMAL BABIES
    xx SEX EDUCATION
ANIMALS
    (subdivided further by name of animal)
    see also KINDNESS TO ANIMALS
        PETS
——CATS
    x cats
——DOGS
    x dogs
——HORSES
    x horses
animals—mythological see MYTHOLOGY
animals—prehistoric see PREHISTORIC LIFE
ANIMALS AS PEOPLE
animals in design see DESIGN—ANIMAL
anthropology see RACES OF MAN
ANTIQUITIES
    see also EGYPT—ANCIENT
        GREECE—ANCIENT
        ROME—ANCIENT
    x mummies
      ruins
    xx ARCHAEOLOGY
AQUARIUMS
AQUEDUCTS
ARBOR DAY
    xx HOLIDAYS
ARCHAEOLOGY
    see also ANTIQUITIES
ARCHITECTURAL DETAILS
ARCHITECTURE
    (subdivided further by adjective of country)

ARCHITECTURE (continued)
see also ABBEYS
CASTLES
CATHEDRALS
CHURCHES
HOUSES
MONASTERIES
MOSQUES
OPERA HOUSES
PALACES
SEVEN WONDERS OF THE WORLD
SYNAGOGUES
TEMPLES
——BAROQUE
——GOTHIC
——PRE-COLUMBIAN
——RENAISSANCE
——ROCOCO
——ROMANESQUE
——19th CENTURY
——20th CENTURY
x skyscrapers
arithmetic see MATHEMATICS
Armistice Day see VETERAN'S DAY
ARMOR
ARMY
(subdivided by adjective of country)
x soldiers
uniforms
xx COSTUME—MILITARY
——UNITED STATES
ART
includes painting when artist unknown
(subdivided further by adjective of country)

see also BLOCK PRINTS
DESIGN
DRAWINGS
ENGRAVINGS
ETCHINGS
LITHOGRAPHY
PAINTINGS
SCULPTURE
SILK SCREEN PRINTING
x graphic arts
——AMERICAN
——BAROQUE
——EARLY CHRISTIAN
——INDIAN, AMERICAN
xx INDIANS
——INDIAN, EAST
——JAPANESE
x Japanese prints
——PRE-COLUMBIAN
——PREHISTORIC
——PRIMITIVE
——RENAISSANCE
——ROCOCO
art by children see CHILDREN AS ARTISTS

ART FORGERIES AND THEFTS

art galleries see MUSEUMS AND GALLERIES

ART TECHNIQUES
see also DRAWING TECHNIQUES
PAINTING TECHNIQUES
ARTILLERY
x guns
xx WEAPONS

ARTISTS
unidentified artists at work; also portraits when two or more are on a page
see also CHILDREN AS ARTISTS
SCULPTORS
biography file
astrology see ZODIAC
astronauts see SPACE FLIGHT
ASTRONOMY
x planets
satellites
solar system
stars
sun
xx OBSERVATORIES
SCIENCE
——MOON
x moon
ASYLUMS
xx MENTAL HEALTH
ATOMIC ENERGY
x nuclear energy
AUTOMATION
AUTOMOBILE RACING
x racing
AUTOMOBILES
x buses
cars
trucks
xx DRIVER EDUCATION
TRANSPORTATION
WHEELS
AUTUMN
see also HARVESTS
x fall
seasons

Aztecs see INDIANS—AZTECS
babies see CHILDREN—BABIES
BACTERIOLOGY
x germs
micro-organisms
ballet see DANCE—BALLET
balloons see AERONAUTICS
TOYS
BAMBOO
xx GRAINS AND GRASSES
BANKS
BARBERS
baseball see SPORTS—BASEBALL
basketball see SPORTS—BASKETBALL
BASKETRY
beach see SEASHORE
BEAUTY CULTURE
x cosmetics
bedtime see FAMILY LIFE
HEALTH
BEEKEEPING
BELLS
BEVERAGES
see also COCOA
COFFEE
TEA
xx FOOD
BIBLE—NEW TESTAMENT
see also CHRISTMAS—NATIVITY
——OLD TESTAMENT
xx COSTUME—BIBLICAL
bicycles see CYCLES AND CYCLING
binoculars see OPTICAL INSTRUMENTS
BIOLOGY
xx SCIENCE

BIRD EGGS AND HATCHING
x eggs
hatching
BIRD HOUSES AND NESTS
x nests
BIRDS
(subdivided by name of bird)
x ducks (wild)
flight
geese (wild)
turkeys (wild)
BLACK HISTORY
see also geography file: AFRICA
biography file
x Afro-Americans
Negroes
xx MINORITIES
BLACKSMITHS
xx OCCUPATIONS
BLIND
xx HANDICAPPED
BLOCK PRINTS
x linoleum cuts
wood engravings
woodcuts
xx ART
blueprints see TECHNICAL DRAWING
BOATS AND SHIPS
see also CANOEING
SHIP BUILDING
SHIPWRECKS
x ships
xx TRANSPORTATION
——SAIL

x sailing
——STEAM
x steamboats and steamships
BODY
the human body
x anatomy
ear
eye
growth (human)
hands
human body
physiology
skeleton
xx SCIENCE
SEX EDUCATION
book illustrations see ILLUSTRATIONS
BOOK PLATES
BOOKS AND READING
x reading
xx SCHOOLS
BOTANY
see also FLOWERS AND PLANTS
TREES
xx SCIENCE
boxes see PACKAGING
Boy Scouts see SCOUTING
boys see CHILDREN
YOUTH
boxing see SPORTS—BOXING
BREAD
xx FOOD
BRIDGES
see also VIADUCTS
BROTHERHOOD

BUILDING CONSTRUCTION
  x construction
    house painting
BULL FIGHTING
  x matadors
BUOYS
buses see AUTOMOBILES
business skills see OFFICE SKILLS
butchers see MEAT

cabinet making see CARPENTRY
cacao see COCOA
cafes see RESTAURANTS
CALENDARS
Campfire Girls see SCOUTING
CAMPHOR
CAMPING
  see also SCOUTING
CANOEING
  xx BOATS AND SHIPS
CANALS
CANDLES
CANDY
  xx FOOD
careers see OCCUPATIONS
CARICATURES
  xx CARTOONS
carnivals see FAIRS
        FESTIVALS
CARPENTRY
  x cabinet making
    woodworking
  xx OCCUPATIONS
carpets see RUGS

CARRIAGES AND WAGONS
x wagons
xx TRANSPORTATION
WHEELS
cars see AUTOMOBILES
CARTOONS
see also CARICATURES
x comics
CARVINGS
see also FIGUREHEADS
TOTEM POLES
x wood carvings
xx SCULPTURE
CASTLES
(subdivided by adjective of country)
xx ARCHITECTURE
CATHEDRALS
(subdivided by adjective of country)
xx ARCHITECTURE
cats see ANIMALS—CATS
CAVES
cement see CONCRETE
CEMETERIES
CERAMICS
(subdivided by adjective of country)
x clay
porcelain
pottery
Chanukah see HANUKKAH
CHARITY
x Red Cross
Salvation Army
CHARTS AND GRAPHS
x graphs

CHEMISTRY
    xx SCIENCE
CHERUBS
chickens see POULTRY
CHILD LABOR
CHILDREN
    see also FAMILY LIFE
      x boys
        girls
——BABIES
      x babies
CHILDREN AS ARTISTS
      x art by children
    xx ARTISTS
CHILDREN AT PLAY
      x play
CHILDREN IN FOREIGN COUNTRIES
children in school see SCHOOLS
Chinese-Americans see MINORITIES
chivalry see MIDDLE AGES
chocolate see COCOA
choirs see SINGING
CHRISTMAS
    xx HOLIDAYS
——NATIVITY
    xx BIBLE—NEW TESTAMENT
CHURCHES
    (subdivided by adjective of country)
    xx ARCHITECTURE
cinema see MOVING PICTURES
CIRCUS
      x acrobats
——CLOWNS
      x clowns

city life see COMMUNITY LIFE
CITY PLANNING
classrooms see COLLEGES AND UNIVERSITIES
SCHOOLS
clay see CERAMICS
HANDICRAFTS
SCULPTURE
climate see WEATHER
CLOCKS AND WATCHES
x time
watches
clothing see COSTUME
CLOUDS
xx WEATHER
clowns see CIRCUS—CLOWNS
COAL
xx MINING
COAST GUARD
coats of arms see HERALDRY
COCK FIGHTING
COCOA
x cacao
chocolate
xx BEVERAGES
COFFEE
xx BEVERAGES
COINS AND CURRENCY
x currency
college students see COLLEGES AND UNIVERSITIES
COLLEGES AND UNIVERSITIES
(subdivided by name of institution)
x college students
classrooms
students

COLLEGES AND UNIVERSITIES (continued)
x teachers and teaching
universities
xx SCHOOLS
——FOREIGN
COLOR
includes elementary samples of color as well as color studies
COLUMBUS DAY
see also EXPLORATIONS—COLUMBUS
biography file
xx HOLIDAYS
COMBAT—HAND TO HAND
includes dueling but not fencing as a sport
see also JUDO AND KARATE
x dueling
fighting hand to hand
hand to hand combat
comics see CARTOONS
COMMUNICATIONS
includes more than one kind in a picture and history
see also MOVING PICTURES
NEWSPAPERS
RADIO
TELEGRAPH
TELEPHONE
TELEVISION
COMMUNITY LIFE
see also OCCUPATIONS
x city life
ghettoes
inner city
street scenes
subways
urban life
xx ROADS AND STREETS
computers see ELECTRONICS

CONCEPTS
large and small; left and right; near and far; up and down, etc.
CONCRETE
x cement
CONFERENCES
CONSERVATION
see also POLLUTION
xx ECOLOGY
construction see BUILDING CONSTRUCTION
consumer education see HOME ECONOMICS
CONVENTS
xx ABBEYS
cooking see FOOD
COPPER
xx MINING
CORAL
xx MARINE LIFE
CORK
CORN
xx FARMING
cosmetics see BEAUTY CULTURE
COSTUME
(subdivided further by adjective of country)
see also DRAWINGS—FASHION
geography file
x clothing
fashion
xx HOME ECONOMICS
——ACADEMIC
——ACCESSORIES
x gloves
hats
shoes
——AMERICAN COLONIAL
xx PILGRIMS

COSTUME (continued)
——BIBLICAL
see also BIBLE
——ECCLESIASTICAL
——EGYPTIAN
xx EGYPT—ANCIENT
——FANCY DRESS
——GREEK
xx GREECE—ANCIENT
——HAWAIIAN
——INDIAN, AMERICAN
xx INDIANS
——INDIAN, EAST
——MEDIEVAL
——MILITARY
see also ARMY
x uniforms
——NAVAL
see also NAVY
x uniforms
——RENAISSANCE
——ROMAN
xx ROME—ANCIENT
——WEDDING
xx WEDDINGS
——17th CENTURY
——18th CENTURY
——19th CENTURY
——20th CENTURY
more than one period on a page
——1900—1919
——1920—1939
——1940—1949
——1950—1959
——1960—1969
——1970—

COTTON
    xx TEXTILES
courts of law see LAW AND LAWYERS
cowboys see WESTERN LIFE
crafts see HANDICRAFTS
CRIME AND CRIMINOLOGY
    see also DELINQUENCY
        PUNISHMENTS
        POLICE
CROSSES
crowds see PEOPLE
CROWNS
CRUSADES
    xx MIDDLE AGES
crustacea see SHELLFISH
currency see COINS AND CURRENCY
CYCLES AND CYCLING
    x bicycles
      motorcycles

DAIRIES
    xx FARMING
DAMS
DANCE
    xx MOVEMENT
——BALLET
    x ballet
——BALLROOM
——CAFE AND THEATRICAL
——NATIONAL
    x folk dancing
——MODERN
day care see SCHOOLS—NURSERY
DEAF
    xx HANDICAPPED

Decoration Day see MEMORIAL DAY
decorations (military) see MEDALS
deep sea diving see DIVING
DELINQUENCY
x juvenile delinquency
xx CRIME AND CRIMINOLOGY
DENTAL MEDICINE
x teeth
xx HEALTH
OCCUPATIONS
DESERTS
DESIGN
(subdivided further by adjective of country)
xx ART
——ANIMAL
x animals in design
——BORDER
——INDIAN, AMERICAN
xx INDIANS
——NATURE
x moon
nature in design
sun
wind
——PENNSYLVANIA DUTCH
DEVILS
dirigibles see AERONAUTICS
DISEASES
x venereal diseases
xx MEDICINE
SEX EDUCATION
DIVING
diving with apparatus
see also SPORTS—DIVING AND SWIMMING
x deep sea diving
skin diving

docks see WHARVES AND DOCKS
doctors see MEDICINE
dogs see ANIMALS—DOGS
DOLLS
    xx TOYS
DRAGONS
    xx MYTHOLOGY
drama see THEATER
drawing—technical see TECHNICAL DRAWING
DRAWING TECHNIQUES
    xx ART TECHNIQUES
DRAWINGS
    (subdivided further by name of artist)
    xx ART
——ANIMALS AND BIRDS
——FASHION
    x fashion
    xx COSTUME
——FIGURE
——GOGH
——HEADS
——LEONARDO
——REMBRANDT
dressing and undressing see SKILLS
DRIVER EDUCATION
    see also AUTOMOBILES
    x road signs
      traffic signs
    xx SIGNS AND SYMBOLS
drugs see MEDICINE
          NARCOTICS
drug stores see STORES
ducks (domestic) see POULTRY
ducks (wild) see BIRDS

dueling see COMBAT HAND TO HAND
DWARFS AND MIDGETS
    x midgets
DYEING

ear see BODY
earth science see GEOLOGY
EARTHQUAKES
EASTER
    xx HOLIDAYS
ECOLOGY
    see also CONSERVATION
        POLLUTION
    x environment
eggs see BIRD EGGS AND HATCHING
    FOOD
    REPTILES
EGYPT—ANCIENT
    see also COSTUME—EGYPTIAN
    xx ANTIQUITIES
        HISTORY—ANCIENT
elections see GOVERNMENT
ELECTRICITY AND MAGNETISM
    x magnetism
    xx SCIENCE
ELECTRONICS
    x computers
ELEVATORS
ELVES AND FAIRIES
    x fairies
        gnomes
    xx ILLUSTRATIONS—FAIRY TALES

EMBLEMS
    xx SIGNS AND SYMBOLS
embroidery see NEEDLEWORK
emigration see IMMIGRATION AND EMIGRATION
EMOTIONS
ENAMELS
ENGINEERING
engines see MACHINERY
ENGRAVINGS
    xx ART
environment see ECOLOGY
    NATURE STUDY
    POLLUTION
ESKIMOS
    see also geography file: POLAR REGIONS
ETCHINGS
    xx ART
ETIQUETTE
    x manners
EXPLORATIONS
    (subdivided further by name of explorer)
——COLUMBUS
    xx COLUMBUS DAY
EXPLOSIVES
EXPOSITIONS
    (subdivided by name of city)
    x world's fairs
    xx FAIRS
eye see BODY
EYEGLASSES
    xx OPTICAL INSTRUMENTS

FACTORIES
    see also TEXTILES

FACTORIES (continued)
x industries
manufacturing
fairies see ELVES AND FAIRIES
fairy tales see ILLUSTRATIONS—FAIRY TALES
FAIRS
see also EXPOSITIONS
x carnivals
fall see AUTUMN
FAMILY LIFE
x bedtime
fathers
grandparents
mothers
xx CHILDREN
HOME ECONOMICS
SEX EDUCATION
FANS
hand-held fans
farm life see FARMING
FARMING
see also CORN
DAIRIES
HARVESTS
POULTRY
STOCK RAISING
WHEAT
x agriculture
farm life
fashion see COSTUME
DRAWINGS—FASHION
FATHER'S DAY
x fathers
xx HOLIDAYS
fathers see FAMILY LIFE
FATHER'S DAY

fencing see SPORTS
FESTIVALS
    x carnivals
fighting hand to hand see COMBAT—HAND TO HAND
FIGUREHEADS
    xx CARVINGS
FIREARMS
    x guns
    xx WEAPONS
FIRES AND FIREMEN
    xx OCCUPATIONS
FIREWORKS
FIRST AID
    see also LIFE SAVING
    xx MEDICINE
FISH
    (subdivided by name of fish)
    xx MARINE LIFE
FISHING
——COMMERCIAL
    xx OCCUPATIONS
FLAG DAY
    xx HOLIDAYS
FLAGS
    (subdivided further by adjective of country)
——STATE
    x state flags
flax see LINEN
flight see AERONAUTICS
        BIRDS
FLOODS
FLOWER ARRANGEMENT
FLOWERS AND PLANTS
    (subdivided by name of flower or plant)

FLOWERS AND PLANTS (continued)
see also GRAINS AND GRASSES
MOSS
TREES
x plants
xx BOTANY
——STATE
x state flowers
flying saucers see SPACE FLIGHT
folk dancing see DANCE—NATIONAL
FOOD
see also BEVERAGES
BREAD
CANDY
FRUIT
MEAT
NUTS
VEGETABLES
x cooking
eggs
nutrition
xx HOME ECONOMICS
football see SPORTS—FOOTBALL
FORESTRY
FORMS OF LAND AND WATER
see also GLACIERS
MOUNTAINS
RIVERS AND STREAMS
x icebergs
lakes
FORTS
FORTUNE-TELLING
FOSSILS
x petrified wood
FOUNTAINS

FOURTH OF JULY
  x Independence Day
  xx HOLIDAYS
fowl see POULTRY
fox hunting see HUNTING
frogs see AMPHIBIANS
FRUIT
  (subdivided by name of fruit)
  xx FOOD
FRUIT GROWING
FUNERALS
FUNGI
FURNITURE
  (subdivided further by adjective of country, period and article of furniture)
  see also HOUSES—INTERIORS
  xx HOME ECONOMICS
——AMERICAN COLONIAL
——ANCIENT
——BEDS
——CHAIRS
——OUTDOOR
——TABLES
FURS AND FUR TRADE

galleries see MUSEUMS AND GALLERIES
games see AMUSEMENTS AND GAMES
Games—Olympic see OLYMPIC GAMES
garbage disposal see REFUSE AND REFUSE DISPOSAL
GARDENING
  see also NURSERIES—HORTICULTURAL
GARDENS
——JAPANESE

gasoline see PETROLEUM
geese (domestic) see POULTRY
geese (wild) see BIRDS
GEMS
GEOLOGY
    see also ROCKS
     x earth science
    xx SCIENCE
geometry see MATHEMATICS
George Washington's Birthday see WASHINGTON'S
  BIRTHDAY
germs see BACTERIOLOGY
ghettoes see COMMUNITY LIFE
        SLUMS
GHOSTS
GIANTS
    xx MYTHOLOGY
Girls Scouts see SCOUTING
girls see CHILDREN
      YOUTH
GLACIERS
    xx FORMS OF LAND AND WATER
GLASS
    see also STAINED GLASS
GLOBES
    xx MAPS
gloves see COSTUME—ACCESSORIES
gnomes see ELVES AND FAIRIES
gold see METALWORK
      MINING
GOVERNMENT
     x elections
      politics
GRAINS AND GRASSES

see also BAMBOO
x grasses
xx FLOWERS AND PLANTS
grandparents see FAMILY LIFE
graphic arts see ART
graphs see CHARTS AND GRAPHS
grasses see GRAINS AND GRASSES
GREECE—ANCIENT
see also COSTUME—GREEK
xx ANTIQUITIES
HISTORY—ANCIENT
greenhouses see NURSERIES—HORTICULTURAL
GRINDSTONES
grocers see STORES
ground-hog day see SPRING
growth (human) see BODY
GUIDED MISSILES AND ROCKETS
x missiles
rockets
guns see ARTILLERY
FIREARMS
GYMNASIUMS
GYMNASTICS
x physical education
GYPSIES

HABITATIONS
human
xx HOUSES
HALLOWEEN
xx HOLIDAYS
HANDICAPPED
see also BLIND
DEAF

HANDICRAFTS
see also PAPER SCULPTURE
x clay
crafts
hand to hand combat see COMBAT—HAND TO HAND
hands see BODY
HANUKKAH
x Chanukah
xx HOLIDAYS
JEWS
HARBORS
see also WHARVES AND DOCKS
HARVESTS
xx AUTUMN
FARMING
hatching see BIRD EGGS AND HATCHING
hats see COSTUME—ACCESSORIES
HEADDRESSES
see also MASKS
HEALTH
see also DENTAL MEDICINE
MEDICINE
x bedtime
hygiene
sleep
HEATING
x stoves
helicopters see AERONAUTICS
HEMP
HERALDRY
x coats of arms
HIGHWAYS
xx ROADS AND STREETS
HIKING
see also PATHS AND TRAILS
SCOUTING

HISTORY
see also WAR
geography file for history since the rise of modern nations
HISTORY—ANCIENT
see also EGYPT—ANCIENT
GREECE—ANCIENT
ROME—ANCIENT
x ancient history
history—medieval see MIDDLE AGES
HOLIDAYS
see also ARBOR DAY
CHRISTMAS
COLUMBUS DAY
EASTER
FATHER'S DAY
FLAG DAY
FOURTH OF JULY
HALLOWEEN
HANUKKAH
HUMAN RIGHTS DAY
LABOR DAY
LINCOLN'S BIRTHDAY
MAY DAY
MEMORIAL DAY
MOTHER'S DAY
NEW YEAR'S DAY
SAINT PATRICK'S DAY
THANKSGIVING
VALENTINE'S DAY
VETERAN'S DAY
WASHINGTON'S BIRTHDAY
HOME ECONOMICS
see also COSTUME
FAMILY LIFE

HOME ECONOMICS (continued)
FOOD
FURNITURE
HOUSES—INTERIORS
NEEDLEWORK
TABLE DECORATIONS AND SETTINGS
x consumer education
housekeeping
HORSE RACING
x racing
xx SPORTS
horses see ANIMALS—HORSES
HOSPITALS
xx MEDICINE
NURSING
HOTELS AND INNS
x inns
motels
house painting see BUILDING CONSTRUCTION
housekeeping see HOME ECONOMICS
HOUSES
see also HABITATIONS
xx ARCHITECTURE
HOUSES—HISTORIC
——INTERIORS
xx HOME ECONOMICS
FURNITURE
HOUSING
human body see BODY
HUMAN RIGHTS DAY
xx HOLIDAYS
HUNTING
x fox hunting
hygiene see HEALTH

ICE
icebergs see FORMS OF LAND AND WATER
ice skating see SPORTS
illuminated manuscripts see MANUSCRIPTS
ILLUSTRATIONS
(subdivided further by author and then title)
see also MYTHOLOGY
NURSERY RHYMES
x book illustrations
literature
——ARABIAN NIGHTS
——FAIRY TALES
see also ELVES AND FAIRIES
x fairy tales
ILLUSTRATORS
(subdivided by name of illustrator)
IMMIGRATION AND EMIGRATION
x emigration
Incas see INDIANS—INCAS
Independence Day see FOURTH OF JULY
INDIANS
Indians of the Americas
(subdivided further by name of tribe)
see also ART—INDIAN, AMERICAN
COSTUME—INDIAN, AMERICAN
DESIGN—INDIAN, AMERICAN
——AZTECS
x Aztecs
——CEREMONIES
——FARMING
——FAMILY LIFE
——FOOD
——HABITATIONS
——HANDICRAFTS

INDIANS (continued)
——HUNTING
——INCAS
x Incas
——MAYAS
x Mayas
——WARFARE
——WRITING
——13th—19th CENTURIES
——20th CENTURY
xx MINORITIES
industries see FACTORIES
inner city see COMMUNITY LIFE
inns see HOTELS AND INNS
INSECTS
includes arachnids and myriapods
(subdivided further by name of insect)
x scorpions
spiders
——BUTTERFLIES
INTEGRATION AND SEGREGATION
x segregation
interplanetary flight see SPACE FLIGHT
INVENTIONS
IRON AND STEEL
x steel
IRRIGATION
IVORY

Japanese-Americans see MINORITIES
Japanese prints see ART—JAPANESE
JEWELRY
JEWS
see also HANUKKAH
x Purim

Rosh Hashanah
Yom Kippur
xx MINORITIES
RELIGIONS
JUDO AND KARATE
x karate
xx COMBAT—HAND TO HAND
JUNGLES AND RAIN FORESTS
x rain forests
tropical rain forests
juvenile delinquency see DELINQUENCY

karate see JUDO AND KARATE
KEYS AND LOCKS
x locks
kindergarten see SCHOOLS—NURSERY
KINDNESS TO ANIMALS
xx ANIMALS
KITES
knights see MIDDLE AGES
KOREAN WAR
xx WAR

LABOR
LABOR DAY
xx HOLIDAYS
LABORATORIES
LACE
LACQUER
lakes see FORMS OF LAND AND WATER
see also geography file, by name of country
lamps see LIGHTING
LASERS AND MASERS
x masers

LAW AND LAWYERS
x courts of law
xx OCCUPATIONS
lead see MINING
LEAGUE OF NATIONS
LEATHER
LEAVES
see also TREES
lenses see OPTICAL INSTRUMENTS
LETTERS
letters of the Roman alphabet, also monograms
see also WRITING—HISTORY
x alphabets
monograms
levers see MACHINES
LIBRARIES
LIFE SAVING
xx FIRST AID
LIGHTHOUSES
LIGHTING
x lamps
LIGHTNING
LINCOLN'S BIRTHDAY
see also biography file
x Abraham Lincoln's Birthday
xx HOLIDAYS
LINEN
x flax
xx TEXTILES
linoleum cuts see BLOCK PRINTS
literature see ILLUSTRATIONS
LITHOGRAPHY
xx ART
——CURRIER AND IVES
lizards see REPTILES

LOADING AND UNLOADING
x unloading
locks see KEYS AND LOCKS
LUMBERING
xx OCCUPATIONS
WOOD

MACHINERY
x engines
MACHINES
simple machines, levers, pulleys
x levers
pulleys
xx PHYSICS
MADONNAS
xx PAINTINGS
MAGIC
magnetism see ELECTRICITY AND MAGNETISM
mailmen see POSTAL SERVICE
man—prehistoric see PREHISTORIC LIFE
manners see ETIQUETTE
manufacturing see FACTORIES
MANUSCRIPTS
x illuminated manuscripts
MAPS
(subdivided further by name of country)
see also GLOBES
——WORLD
marble see ROCKS
QUARRYING
MARINE CORPS
MARINE LIFE
see also CORAL
FISH
SHELLFISH

MARINE LIFE (continued)
SPONGES
x sea life
marine studies see PAINTINGS—SEASCAPES
MARIONETTES AND PUPPETS
x puppets
MARITIME TRADES
x merchant marines
xx OCCUPATIONS
MARKETS
xx STORES
MARQUETRY
masers see LASERS AND MASERS
MASKS
xx HEADDRESSES
matadors see BULL FIGHTING
MATHEMATICS
Arabic and Roman numerals, illustrations of mathematical concepts on all levels, and pictures which illustrate elementary numbers such as two books, three dogs, etc.
x abacuses
arithmetic
geometry
numbers
MAY DAY
xx HOLIDAYS
Mayas see INDIANS—MAYAS
measures see WEIGHTS AND MEASURES
MEAT
x butchers
xx FOOD
mechanical drawing see TECHNICAL DRAWING
MEDALS
x decorations (military)
MEDICINE
see also DISEASES

FIRST AID
HOSPITALS
NURSING
x doctors
drugs
pharmacies
xx HEALTH
OCCUPATIONS
medieval history see MIDDLE AGES
MEMORIAL DAY
x Decoration Day
xx HOLIDAYS
memorials see MONUMENTS AND MEMORIALS
MENTAL HEALTH
see also ASYLUMS
merchant marines see MARITIME TRADES
MERMAIDS
xx MYTHOLOGY
merry-go-rounds see AMUSEMENT PARKS
METAL
METALWORK
x gold
pewter
silver
wrought iron
METALSHOP
meteorology see WEATHER
Mexican-Americans see MINORITIES
micro-organisms see BACTERIOLOGY
MICROSCOPES
MIDDLE AGES
see also CRUSADES
x chivalry
history—medieval

MIDDLE AGES (continued)
knights
medieval history
tournaments
midgets see DWARFS AND MIDGETS
MILLS
x watermills
windmills
MINERALS
MINIATURES
xx PAINTINGS
MINING
see also COAL
COPPER
x gold
lead
silver
xx OCCUPATIONS
MINORITIES
see also BLACK HISTORY
INDIANS—20th CENTURY
JEWS
RELIGIONS
geography file:
UNITED STATES—PEOPLE
x Chinese-Americans
Japanese-Americans
Mexican-Americans
Puerto Ricans
MIRAGES
missiles see GUIDED MISSILES AND ROCKETS
MISSIONS
MODELS
x ship models
MONASTERIES

xx ABBEYS
ARCHITECTURE
monograms see LETTERS
MONSTERS
see also SEA SERPENTS
MONUMENTS AND MEMORIALS
see also TOMBS
x memorials
tombstones
moon see ASTRONOMY—MOON
DESIGN—NATURE
MOSAICS
MOSQUES
xx ARCHITECTURE
MOSS
xx FLOWERS AND PLANTS
motels see HOTELS AND INNS
Mother Goose see NURSERY RHYMES
MOTHER'S DAY
x mothers
xx HOLIDAYS
mothers see FAMILY LIFE
MOTHER'S DAY
motorcycles see CYCLES AND CYCLING
MOUNTAINEERING
MOUNTAINS
see also geography file
xx FORMS OF LAND AND WATER
MOVEMENT
human movement
see also DANCE
SPORTS
x action
MOVING PICTURES
(subdivided by name of film)

MOVING PICTURES (continued)
x cinema
xx COMMUNICATIONS
mummies see ANTIQUITIES
murals see PAINTINGS—MURALS
MUSEUMS AND GALLERIES
(subdivided further by adjective of country)
x art galleries
galleries
——UNITED STATES
MUSIC
People playing instruments, conducting or listening; also portraits of musicians when two or more are on a page
see also ORGAN GRINDERS
SINGING
x orchestras
MUSICAL INSTRUMENTS
(subdivided further by name of instrument)
——ANCIENT
MYTHOLOGY
see also DRAGONS
GIANTS
MERMAIDS
x animals—mythological
xx ILLUSTRATIONS
——GREEK AND ROMAN
——NORSE

NARCOTICS
x drugs
nature in design see DESIGN—NATURE
NATURE STUDY
people studying nature outdoors
x environment
xx SCIENCE
NAVIGATION

——INSTRUMENTS
NAVY
(subdivided by adjective of country)
x sailors
uniforms
xx COSTUME—NAVAL
——UNITED STATES
NEEDLEWORK
see also TAILORING
x embroidery
sewing
xx HOME ECONOMICS
Negroes see BLACK HISTORY
nests see BIRD HOUSES AND NESTS
NEW YEAR'S DAY
x time
xx HOLIDAYS
NEWSPAPERS
xx COMMUNICATIONS
NIGHT
NORSEMEN
x Vikings
nuclear energy see ATOMIC ENERGY
numbers see MATHEMATICS
NURSERIES—HORTICULTURAL
x greenhouses
xx GARDENING
NURSERY RHYMES
x Mother Goose
xx ILLUSTRATIONS
nursery schools see SCHOOLS—NURSERY
NURSING
see also HOSPITALS
x uniforms

NURSING (continued)
    xx MEDICINE
        OCCUPATIONS
nutrition see FOOD
NUTS
    xx FOOD

OBSERVATORIES
    see also ASTRONOMY
        TELESCOPES
OCCUPATIONS
    see also BLACKSMITHS
        CARPENTRY
        DENTAL MEDICINE
        FIRES AND FIREMEN
        FISHING—COMMERCIAL
        LAW AND LAWYERS
        LUMBERING
        MARITIME TRADES
        MEDICINE
        MINING
        NURSING
        OFFICE SKILLS
        PLUMBERS
        POLICE
        POSTAL SERVICE
        REFUSE AND REFUSE DISPOSAL
        SHOEMAKING
        SURVEYING
        TAILORING
        VETERINARY MEDICINE
        WHALING
    x careers
        trades
        vocations

OCCUPATIONS (continued)
    xx COMMUNITY LIFE
OCEANOGRAPHY
    xx SCIENCE
OCEANS
        x sea
OFFICE SKILLS
        x business skills
    xx OCCUPATIONS
OFFICES AND OFFICE EQUIPMENT
        x typewriters
oil see PETROLEUM
        WHALING
OLD AGE
OLYMPIC GAMES
        x Games—Olympic
    xx SPORTS
OPERA HOUSES
    xx ARCHITECTURE
OPERAS
OPTICAL ILLUSIONS
OPTICAL INSTRUMENTS
    see also EYEGLASSES
        TELESCOPES
        x binoculars
        lenses
orchestras see MUSIC
ORGAN GRINDERS
    xx MUSIC

PACKAGING
        x boxes
PAINTING TECHNIQUES
    xx ART TECHNIQUES

PAINTINGS
(subdivided further by name of artist)
see also MADONNAS
MINIATURES
xx ART
——GOGH
——LEONARDO
——MICHELANGELO
——MURALS
x murals
——REMBRANDT
——SEASCAPES
x marine studies
seascapes
——SYMBOLIC
x symbolic pictures
——WATERCOLORS
x watercolors
PALACES
(subdivided by adjective of country)
xx ARCHITECTURE
parachutes see AERONAUTICS
PAPER
PAPER SCULPTURE
xx HANDICRAFTS
PARADES
PARKS AND PLAYGROUNDS
x playgrounds
PARTIES
PASSION PLAYS
PATHS AND TRAILS
x trails
xx HIKING
ROADS AND STREETS
PEARL FISHING

PEAT
PEDDLERS
PEOPLE
crowds; groups of adults or adults with children
x crowds
PERFUME
petrified wood see FOSSILS
PETROLEUM
x gasoline
oil
PETS
xx ANIMALS
pewter see METALWORK
pharmacies see MEDICINE
STORES
PHONOGRAPHS
PHOTOGRAPHY
physical education see GYMNASTICS
SPORTS
PHYSICS
see also MACHINES
xx SCIENCE
physiology see BODY
PICNICS
piers see WHARVES AND DOCKS
PILGRIMS
see also COSTUME—AMERICAN COLONIAL
THANKSGIVING
geography file: UNITED STATES—
HISTORY—1603-1764
x Puritans
PIONEERS
PIRATES
planes see AIRPLANES
planets see ASTRONOMY

PLANTATION LIFE
    xx SLAVERY
plants see FLOWERS AND PLANTS
plastics see SYNTHETICS
play see CHILDREN AT PLAY
playgrounds see PARKS AND PLAYGROUNDS
PLUMBERS
    xx OCCUPATIONS
POLICE
    xx CRIME AND CRIMINOLOGY
        OCCUPATIONS
politics see GOVERNMENT
POLLUTION
    x air pollution
        environment
    xx CONSERVATION
        ECOLOGY
pony express see POSTAL SERVICE
porcelain see CERAMICS
POSTAGE STAMPS
    x stamps
POSTAL SERVICE
    x mailmen
        pony express
    xx OCCUPATIONS
POSTERS
    xx ADVERTISING
pottery see CERAMICS
POULTRY
    x chickens
        ducks (domestic)
        fowl
        geese (domestic)
        turkeys (domestic)
    xx FARMING

POVERTY
see also SLUMS
PREHISTORIC LIFE
x animals—prehistoric
man—prehistoric
PRESIDENTS
collective pictures of United States presidents
see also biography file
PRINTING
PRISONS
xx PUNISHMENTS
public speaking see SPEECH
Puerto Ricans see MINORITIES
pulleys see MACHINES
pumps see WATER SUPPLY
PUNISHMENTS
see also PRISONS
xx CRIME AND CRIMINOLOGY
puppets see MARIONETTES AND PUPPETS
Purim see JEWS
Puritans see PILGRIMS
RELIGIONS

QUARRYING
x marble

RACES OF MAN
x anthropology
racing see AUTOMOBILE RACING
HORSE RACING
SPORTS—TRACK AND FIELD
RADAR
RADIO
xx COMMUNICATIONS

RADIUM
RAILROADS
x trains
xx TRANSPORTATION
WHEELS
rain see WEATHER
rain forests see JUNGLES AND RAIN FORESTS
RAINBOWS
xx WEATHER
ranch life see WESTERN LIFE
reading see BOOKS AND READING
Red Cross see CHARITY
REFLECTIONS
REFRIGERATION
REFUGEES
REFUSE AND REFUSE DISPOSAL
x garbage disposal
xx OCCUPATIONS
REHABILITATION
RELIGIONS
see also JEWS
x Puritans
xx MINORITIES
RELIGIOUS ARTICLES
REPTILES
(subdivided by name of reptile)
x alligators
eggs
lizards
snakes
resin see TURPENTINE AND RESIN
RESTAURANTS
x cafes
RICE

RIVERS AND STREAMS
see also geography file
x streams
xx FORMS OF LAND AND WATER
road signs see DRIVER EDUCATION
ROADS AND STREETS
see also HIGHWAYS
COMMUNITY LIFE
PATHS AND TRAILS
x streets
ROBOTS
rockets see GUIDED MISSILES AND ROCKETS
ROCKS
x marble
xx GEOLOGY
rodeos see WESTERN LIFE
ROME—ANCIENT
see also COSTUME—ROMAN
xx ANTIQUITIES
HISTORY—ANCIENT
ROPE
Rosh Hashanah see JEWS
RUBBER
RUGS
x carpets
——ORIENTAL
ruins see ANTIQUITIES

SAFETY
sailing see BOATS AND SHIPS—SAIL
sailors see NAVY
SAINT PATRICK'S DAY
xx HOLIDAYS

SAINTS
SALT
Salvation Army see CHARITY
SAND
satellites see ASTRONOMY
                SPACE FLIGHT
scales see WEIGHTS AND MEASURES
SCHOOLS
    see also BOOKS AND READING
                COLLEGES AND UNIVERSITIES
      x children in school
        classrooms
        students
        teachers and teaching
——FOREIGN
——HISTORIC
——MILITARY
——NURSERY
      x day care
        kindergarten
        nursery schools
——RURAL
SCIENCE
  includes portraits of scientists when two or more are on a page
    see also ASTRONOMY
                BIOLOGY
                BODY
                BOTANY
                CHEMISTRY
                GEOLOGY
                ELECTRICITY AND MAGNETISM
                NATURE STUDY
                OCEANOGRAPHY
                PHYSICS
scorpions see INSECTS

SCOUTING
x Boy Scouts
Campfire Girls
Girl Scouts
xx CAMPING
HIKING
SCREENS
SCULPTORS
unidentified sculptors at work; also portraits when two or more are on a page
see also biography file
xx ARTISTS
SCULPTURE
(subdivided further by adjective of country and name of sculptor)
see also CARVINGS
x clay
xx ART
——MICHELANGELO
——INDIAN, EAST
sea see OCEANS
SEASHORE
sea life see MARINE LIFE
SEA SERPENTS
xx MONSTERS
SEALS
state seals, etc.
x state seals
seascapes see PAINTINGS—SEASCAPES
SEASHORE
x beach
sea
seasons see AUTUMN
SPRING
SUMMER
WINTER

SEEDS
segregation see INTEGRATION AND SEGREGATION
SEVEN WONDERS OF THE WORLD
xx ARCHITECTURE
SEWERS
drains
sewing see NEEDLEWORK
TAILORING
SEX EDUCATION
see also ANIMAL BABIES
BODY
DISEASES
FAMILY LIFE
SHELLFISH
x crustacea
xx MARINE LIFE
SHELLS
ship models see MODELS
SHIP BUILDING
xx BOATS AND SHIPS
ships see BOATS AND SHIPS
SHIPWRECKS
xx BOATS AND SHIPS
SHOEMAKING
xx OCCUPATIONS
shoes see COSTUME—ACCESSORIES
shops see STORES
SIGNS AND SYMBOLS
see also ADVERTISING
DRIVER EDUCATION
EMBLEMS
x symbols
SILHOUETTES
SILK

SILK SCREEN PRINTING
    xx ART
silver see METALWORK
    MINING
    TABLE DECORATIONS AND SETTINGS
SINGING
    x choirs
    xx MUSIC
skating see SPORTS
skeleton see BODY
skiing see SPORTS
SKILLS
    elementary manual skills: buttoning, lacing shoes, pasting, using scissors, etc.
    x dressing and undressing
skin diving see DIVING
skyscrapers see ARCHITECTURE—20th CENTURY
SLAVERY
    see also PLANTATION LIFE
sleep see HEALTH
SLUMS
    x ghettoes
    xx POVERTY
smoking see TOBACCO
SNAILS
SNAKE CHARMERS
snakes see REPTILES
snow see WEATHER
    WINTER
SNOW CRYSTALS
snowmen see WINTER
SOAP
soda fountains see STORES
SOIL
solar system see ASTRONOMY
soldiers see ARMY

SOUND
sound waves; people or things making noise
x acoustics
SPACE FLIGHT
x astronauts
flying saucers
interplanetary flight
satellites
xx AERONAUTICS
SPEECH
x public speaking
SPICES
spiders see INSECTS
SPINNING AND WEAVING
x weaving
SPONGES
xx MARINE LIFE
SPORTING GOODS
x sports equipment
SPORTS
(subdivided further by name of sport)
see also HORSE RACING
OLYMPIC GAMES
x fencing
ice skating
physical education
skating
skiing
tournaments
xx AMUSEMENTS AND GAMES
MOVEMENT
——BASEBALL
x baseball
——BASKETBALL
x basketball

——BOXING
x boxing
——DIVING AND SWIMMING
x swimming
xx DIVING
——FOOTBALL
x football
——TRACK AND FIELD
x racing
sports equipment see SPORTING GOODS
SPRING
x ground-hog day
seasons
STADIUMS
stage see THEATER
STAINED GLASS
xx GLASS
stamps see POSTAGE STAMPS
stars see ASTRONOMY
state flags see FLAGS—STATE
state flowers see FLOWERS AND PLANTS—STATE
state seals see SEALS
steamboats and steamships see BOATS AND SHIPS—STEAM
steel see IRON AND STEEL
STOCK RAISING
see also WESTERN LIFE
xx FARMING
STORES
see also MARKETS
x drug stores
grocers
pharmacies
shops
soda fountains

storms see WEATHER
stoves see HEATING
streams see RIVERS AND STREAMS
street scenes see COMMUNITY LIFE
streets see ROADS AND STREETS
students see COLLEGES AND UNIVERSITIES
SCHOOLS
subways see COMMUNITY LIFE
SUGAR
beet, cane, maple
SUMMER
x seasons
SUMMERHOUSES
sun see ASTRONOMY
DESIGN—NATURE
SUNDIALS
x time
SUNRISE
SUNSET
SURVEYING
xx OCCUPATIONS
swimming see SPORTS—DIVING AND SWIMMING
swords see WEAPONS
symbolic pictures see PAINTINGS—SYMBOLIC
symbols see SIGNS AND SYMBOLS
SYNAGOGUES
xx ARCHITECTURE
SYNTHETICS
x plastics

TABLE DECORATIONS AND SETTINGS
x silver
xx HOME ECONOMICS

TAILORING
x sewing
xx NEEDLEWORK
OCCUPATIONS
TAPESTRIES
TATTOOING
TAXIDERMY
TEA
xx BEVERAGES
teachers and teaching see COLLEGES AND
UNIVERSITIES, SCHOOLS
TECHNICAL DRAWING
x blueprints
drawing—technical
mechanical drawing
teenagers see YOUTH
teeth see DENTAL MEDICINE
TELEGRAPH
xx COMMUNICATIONS
TELEPHONE
xx COMMUNICATIONS
TELESCOPES
xx OBSERVATORIES
OPTICAL INSTRUMENTS
TELEVISION
xx COMMUNICATIONS
TEMPLES
xx ARCHITECTURE
TEXTILES
see also COTTON
LINEN
xx FACTORIES
THANKSGIVING
xx HOLIDAYS
PILGRIMS

THEATER
x drama
stage
THRONES
TILES
time see CLOCKS AND WATCHES
NEW YEAR'S DAY
SUNDIALS
toads see AMPHIBIANS
TOBACCO
x smoking
TOMBS
xx MONUMENTS AND MEMORIALS
tombstones see MONUMENTS AND MEMORIALS
TOOLS
tornadoes see WEATHER
TOTEM POLES
xx CARVINGS
tournaments see MIDDLE AGES
SPORTS
TOYS
see also DOLLS
x balloons
trade-marks see ADVERTISING
trades see OCCUPATIONS
traffic signs see DRIVER EDUCATION
trails see PATHS AND TRAILS
trains see RAILROADS
TRANSPORTATION
includes history
see also AERONAUTICS
AIRPLANES
AUTOMOBILES
BOATS AND SHIPS

CARRIAGES AND WAGONS
RAILROADS
TREES
(subdivided by name of tree)
xx BOTANY
FLOWERS AND PLANTS
LEAVES
tropical rain forests see JUNGLES AND RAIN FORESTS
trucks see AUTOMOBILES
TUNNELS
turkeys (domestic) see POULTRY
turkeys (wild) see BIRDS
TURPENTINE AND RESIN
x resin
typewriters see OFFICES AND OFFICE EQUIPMENT

UNICEF see UNITED NATIONS
uniforms see ARMY
COSTUME—MILITARY
COSTUME—NAVAL
NURSING
UNITED NATIONS
x UNICEF
universities see COLLEGES AND UNIVERSITIES
unloading see LOADING AND UNLOADING
urban life see COMMUNITY LIFE

VALENTINE'S DAY
xx HOLIDAYS
VALENTINES

VEGETABLES
(subdivided by name of vegetable)
xx FOOD
VENDING MACHINES
veneral diseases see DISEASES
VETERAN'S DAY
x Armistice Day
xx HOLIDAYS
VETERINARY MEDICINE
xx OCCUPATIONS
VIADUCTS
xx BRIDGES
VIETNAMESE WAR
xx WAR
Vikings see NORSEMEN
VIOLENCE
vocations see OCCUPATIONS
VOLCANOES

wagons see CARRIAGES AND WAGONS
WALLPAPER
WAR
see also KOREAN WAR
VIETNAMESE WAR
WORLD WAR I
WORLD WAR II
geography file, by name of country
xx HISTORY
WASHINGTON'S BIRTHDAY
see also biography file
x George Washington's Birthday
xx HOLIDAYS
watches see CLOCKS AND WATCHES
WATER
includes use

WATER SUPPLY
see also WELLS
x pumps
watercolors see PAINTINGS—WATERCOLORS
WATERFALLS
watermills see MILLS
WEAPONS
see also ARTILLERY
FIREARMS
x swords
WEATHER
see also CLOUDS
RAINBOWS
WINTER
x climate
meteorology
rain
snow
storms
tornadoes
wind
WEATHER VANES
weaving see SPINNING AND WEAVING
WEDDINGS
see also COSTUME—WEDDING
WEIGHTS AND MEASURES
x measures
scales
WELLS
xx WATER SUPPLY
WESTERN LIFE
x cowboys
ranch life
rodeos
xx STOCK RAISING

WHALING
x oil
xx OCCUPATIONS
WHARVES AND DOCKS
x docks
piers
xx HARBORS
WHEAT
xx FARMING
WHEELS
see also AUTOMOBILES
CARRIAGES AND WAGONS
RAILROADS
wind see WEATHER
DESIGN—NATURE
windmills see MILLS
WINTER
x seasons
snow
snowmen
xx WEATHER
WITCHES
WOOD
see also LUMBERING
wood carvings see CARVINGS
wood engravings see BLOCK PRINTS
woodcuts see BLOCK PRINTS
woodworking see CARPENTRY
WOOL
WORLD WAR I
xx WAR
WORLD WAR II
xx WAR
world's fairs see EXPOSITIONS

WORMS
WRITING—HISTORY
includes Roman and non-Roman alphabets

x alphabets
xx LETTERS
wrought iron see METALWORK

X-RAY

YMCA, YMHA, YWCA see YOUTH
Yom Kippur see JEWS
YOUTH
x adolescents
boys
girls
teenagers
YMCA, YMHA, YWCA

ZODIAC
x astrology
ZOOS

II. Geography

This list is intended to include history since the rise of modern nations. Headings may be subdivided by city, history (further subdivided by date) and people.

For maps and for ancient and medieval history, see subject file.

To simplify, RUSSIA is used for the USSR. This list also has separate headings for ARMENIA, LATVIA, ESTONIA, LITHUANIA.

Abyssinia see AFRICA—ETHIOPIA

AFGHANISTAN

AFRICA
general pictures

see also ALGERIA
EGYPT
LIBYA
MOROCCO
TUNISIA

——ANGOLA
x Portuguese West Africa

——BOTSWANA
x Bechuanaland

——BURUNDI
x Urundi

——CAMEROON

——CENTRAL

AFRICA (continued)
——CENTRAL AFRICAN REPUBLIC
  x Ubangi-Shari
——CHAD
——CONGO
  x Brazzaville
    People's Republic of the Congo
——DAHOMEY
——ETHIOPIA
  x Abyssinia
——GABON
——GAMBIA
——GHANA
  x Gold Coast
——GUINEA
  x French Guinea
——IVORY COAST
——KENYA
——LIBERIA
——MALAWI
  x Nyasaland
——MALI
  x Sudanese Republic
——MAURITANIA
——NIGER
——NIGERIA
——RHODESIA
——RWANDA
——SENEGAL
——SIERRA LEONE
——SOMALIA
——SOUTH AFRICA, REPUBLIC OF
  x Union of South Africa
——SOUTHERN RHODESIA
——SUDAN

——SWAZILAND
——TANZANIA
x Tanganyika
Zanzibar
——TOGO
x French Togo
——UGANDA
——UPPER VOLTA
x Voltaic Republic
——ZAIRE
——ZAMBIA
x Northern Rhodesia
ALBANIA
ALGERIA
xx AFRICA
ANDORRA
Antarctic see POLAR REGIONS
Arab Republic see EGYPT
Arctic see POLAR REGIONS
ARGENTINA
ARMENIA
Aruba see NETHERLANDS ANTILLES
Ascension Island see SAINT HELENA
ASIA
general pictures
AUSTRALIA
AUSTRIA
AZORES

BAHAMA ISLANDS
BAHRAIN
BANGLADESH
x Bengal Nation
Barbados see CARIBBEAN ISLANDS

Bechuanaland see AFRICA—BOTSWANA
BELGIUM
Bengal Nation see BANGLADESH
BERMUDA ISLANDS
BHUTAN
BOLIVIA
BRAZIL
Brazzaville see AFRICA—CONGO
British Guiana see GUYANA
BULGARIA
BURMA

CAMBODIA
CANADA
——MONTREAL
——NEWFOUNDLAND
——NOVA SCOTIA
——OTTAWA
——QUEBEC
CANARY ISLANDS
CARIBBEAN ISLANDS
    x Barbados
      Dominican Republic
      Hispaniola
      Leeward Islands
      Tobago
      Virgin Islands
      West Indies
      Windward Islands
——HAITI
    x Haiti
——JAMAICA
    x Jamaica
——TRINIDAD
    x Trinidad

CENTRAL AMERICA
general pictures
CEYLON
CHILE
CHINA
COLOMBIA
COSTA RICA
CUBA
Curaçao see NETHERLANDS ANTILLES
CYPRUS
CZECHOSLOVAKIA

DENMARK
Dominican Republic see CARIBBEAN ISLANDS
Dutch East Indies see INDONESIA

ECUADOR
EGYPT
modern
see also EGYPT—ANCIENT in subject file
x Arab Republic
xx AFRICA
EL SALVADOR
ENGLAND
——HISTORY
——LONDON
ESTONIA
EUROPE
general pictures

FIJI
FINLAND
Formosa see TAIWAN
FRANCE
——HISTORY
——PARIS

French Guinea see AFRICA—GUINEA
French Togo see AFRICA—TOGO

GERMANY
——BERLIN
——HISTORY
GIBRALTAR
Gold Coast see AFRICA—GHANA
GREECE
modern
see also GREECE—ANCIENT in subject file
GREENLAND
GUATEMALA
GUYANA
x British Guiana

Haiti see CARIBBEAN ISLANDS—HAITI
Hispaniola see CARIBBEAN ISLANDS
Holland see NETHERLANDS
HONDURAS
HONG KONG
HUNGARY

ICELAND
INDONESIA
x Dutch East Indies
x Netherlands East Indies
IRAN
x Persia
IRAQ
IRELAND
ISRAEL

ITALY
——ROME
see also ROME—ANCIENT in subject file

Jamaica see CARIBBEAN ISLANDS—JAMAICA
JAPAN
JORDAN
x Transjordan

KOREA
KUWAIT

LAOS
LAPLAND
LATVIA
LEBANON
Leeward Islands see CARIBBEAN ISLANDS
Liberia see AFRICA—LIBERIA
xx AFRICA
LIECHTENSTEIN
LITHUANIA
LUXEMBOURG

MADAGASCAR
MALAY ARCHIPELAGO
x Malaysia
Malaysia see MALAY ARCHIPELAGO
MALTA
Melanesia see SOUTH SEA ISLANDS
MEXICO
——HISTORY
——MEXICO CITY
Micronesia see SOUTH SEA ISLANDS
MONACO

MONGOLIA
MOROCCO
    xx AFRICA

NEPAL
NETHERLANDS
    x Holland
NETHERLANDS ANTILLES
    x Aruba
      Curaçao
Netherlands East Indies see INDONESIA
NEW GUINEA
    x Papua
NEW ZEALAND
NICARAGUA
North Pole see POLAR REGIONS
Northern Rhodesia see AFRICA—ZAMBIA
Nyasaland see AFRICA—MALAWI
NORWAY

Oceania see SOUTH SEA ISLANDS

PAKISTAN
PANAMA
Papua see NEW GUINEA
PARAGUAY
People's Republic of the Congo see AFRICA
    —CONGO
Persia see IRAN
PERU
PHILIPPINES
POLAND
POLAR REGIONS
    see also EXPLORATIONS in subject file

POLAR REGIONS (continued)
x Antarctic
Arctic
North Pole
South Pole
Polynesia see SOUTH SEA ISLANDS
PORTUGAL
Portuguese West Africa see AFRICA—ANGOLA
Puerto Rico see UNITED STATES—
PUERTO RICO

RUMANIA
RUSSIA
x Union of Soviet Socialist Republics
x USSR
——SIBERIA
x Siberia

SAINT HELENA
x Ascension Island
Tristan da Cunha Island
Samoa see SOUTH SEA ISLANDS
SAN MARINO
SAUDI ARABIA
SCOTLAND
Siam see THAILAND
Siberia see RUSSIA—SIBERIA
SINGAPORE
South Africa see AFRICA
SOUTH AMERICA
general pictures
South Pole see POLAR REGIONS
SOUTH SEA ISLANDS
x Melanesia
Micronesia

SOUTH SEA ISLANDS (continued)
Oceania
Polynesia
Samoa
Tahiti
SPAIN
Sudanese Republic see AFRICA—MALI
SWEDEN
SWITZERLAND
SYRIA

Tahiti see SOUTH SEA ISLANDS
TAIWAN
x Formosa
Tanganyika see AFRICA—TANZANIA
TASMANIA
THAILAND
x Siam
TIBET
Tobago see CARIBBEAN ISLANDS
Transjordan see JORDAN
Trinidad see CARIBBEAN ISLANDS—TRINIDAD
Tristan da Cunha Island see SAINT HELENA
TUNISIA
xx AFRICA
TURKEY

Ubangi-Shari see AFRICA—CENTRAL AFRICAN REPUBLIC
Union of South Africa see AFRICA—SOUTH AFRICA, REPUBLIC OF
Union of Soviet Socialist Republics see RUSSIA
UNITED STATES
——GOVERNMENT

——HISTORY
—— ——1000—1509 (DISCOVERY)
—— ——1510—1602 (EXPLORATION)
—— ——1603—1764 (COLONIZATION)
—— ——1765—1788 (REVOLUTION)
—— ——1789—1845
includes War of 1812
—— ——1846—1860
includes Mexican War
—— ——1861—1865
includes Civil War
—— ——1866-1899
includes Reconstruction and Spanish American War
—— ——20th CENTURY
see also subject file for wars, by name of war
——MOUNTAINS
——NATIONAL PARKS
——PEOPLE
——PUERTO RICO
x Puerto Rico
——RIVERS
——STATES A-Z
——WASHINGTON, D.C.
URUGUAY
Urundi see AFRICA—BURUNDI
USSR see RUSSIA

VATICAN CITY
VENEZUELA
VIETNAM
Virgin Islands see CARIBBEAN ISLANDS
Voltaic Republic see AFRICA—UPPER VOLTA

WALES
West Indies see CARIBBEAN ISLANDS

Windward Islands see CARIBBEAN ISLANDS

YEMEN
YUGOSLAVIA

Zanzibar see AFRICA—TANZANIA

Appendix
Other Uses of the Dry Mounting Press

The dry mounting press can do a variety of useful work in the school and library.

It is designed so that it can mount materials larger than the platen. In this case, mounting should be started at the center of the large picture and worked out to the ends. Large pictures should not be tacked to the mount before inserting in the press, since wrinkles may develop if the picture is not free to expand. A heavy sheet of paper such as Kraft wrapping paper should be folded over the print with edges extending out beyond the platen so that no ridge marks will appear on the mounted material.

Some oversized pictures can be placed on two mounts with a hinge made of backing cloth, attached by the press. The hinge must always be applied to the boards in closed position.

The press will also attach backing cloth to make accordion folds, or to add flexible strength to such materials as charts and maps.

Pliable and rigid materials can be laminated with film by the press, to give permanent protection against rips, stains and moisture to materials that get hard use, such as maps, charts and drawings, although, as has been mentioned, this protection given to pictures in a large collection has not proved worth the cost and labor. The laminating film, obtainable in matte or glossy finish, does not grow brittle or yellow with age.

The press can make color or black and white transparencies for use in overhead projectors from almost any picture from a magazine printed on clay-coated paper. Under heat and pressure from the press, a specially prepared film lifts the ink intact from the paper and holds it in permanent bond. The original picture on paper is of course destroyed in this process. A simple test of paper to see if it is clay coated and suitable for making transparencies can be made by rubbing a moistened finger tip over an unprinted spot on the page. Clay coating will leave a white smudge on the finger tip.

For mounting heavier materials, such as album covers or plywood backing for pictures or photographs, the press can be adjusted by loosening the bolts which hold the heating unit to the arms of the press. If additional pressure is wanted for thin materials without the trouble of adjusting bolts, a sheet or two of cardboard can be placed on the pad of the press. For most work going into a picture file, the new press will not need adjusting.

Backing cloth and film for laminating and making transparencies can be obtained from the manufacturer of the dry mounting press, or from most audio-visual supply houses.

With a little experimentation, many uses can be found for the press in making exhibits and bulletin board displays and in reinforcing materials and mounting on wood.

Glossary

Broad heading. A word or group of words chosen to represent an inclusive rather than a specific subject. SEASONS is a broad heading. SPRING is a specific heading.

Card catalog. A file in which each heading is on a separate card arranged in alphabetical or, sometimes, chronological order in a drawer.

Checklist. A list of headings in notebook form, in contrast to a card catalog in which each heading is on a separate card in a file drawer.

Classification. A systematic arrangement of subjects in groups or categories based upon some relationship, in contrast to a *list*, which is usually alphabetical.

Guide card. A card having a label which stands above the file, to indicate arrangement or to aid in locating material in the file.

Heading. See Subject heading.

Manual. A handbook of rules or a concise treatment of the essentials of a subject.

Name authority card. A catalog card that records the name or spelling of the name (where more than one are known) chosen for consistent use in a collection. The card will also list tracings from variations of the name for which there are "see" references in the card catalog.

Reference. A direction from one word or group of words to another or others.

Scope note. A statement defining or indicating the coverage of a heading.

"See also" reference. Directions from a heading which is used to related or more specific headings *also* used.

"See" reference. Directions from a heading which is *not* used to a heading which is used.

Specific heading. A word or group of words chosen to express an individual subject, as distinguished from a broad heading which would cover a class including that subject. SPRING is a specific heading; SEASONS is a broad heading.

Subheading. A division of a subject heading, added to separate the subject into further categories.

Subject heading. A word or group of words chosen to represent a subject, with which all pictures wanted for the same theme in the collection are labeled, and by which the pictures are arranged in the file.

Tracing. The record under a heading of a reference or references made to that heading.

Bibliography

Picture subject heading lists:

Dane, William J. *The Picture Collection Subject Headings.* Sixth Edition. Hamden, Connecticut: The Shoe String Press, 1968.

Ireland, Norma Olin. *The Picture File in School, College and Public Libraries*; Revised and Enlarged Edition. Boston: F. W. Faxon, 1952.

For manufacturers of and dealers in equipment and supplies:

Educator's Purchasing Guide; Media and Methods. Philadelphia: North American Publishing Co. Revised periodically. See latest edition.

"Annual Purchasing Guide" in *Library Journal.* See April issue each year.

For information on house organs and periodicals:

Gebbie House Magazine Directory. New York: Gebbie Press. Revised periodically. See latest edition.

Haycock, Ken. *Free Magazines for Teachers and Libraries 1974.* Toronto, Ontario: Ontario Library Association/School Libraries Division.

Katz, Bill. *Magazines for Libraries; for the General Reader, and School, Junior College, College, and Public Libraries.* New York: R. R. Bowker. Revised periodically. See latest edition.

The Standard Periodical Directory. New York: Oxbridge. Revised periodically. See latest edition.

For lists of free materials:

Bibliographic Index; a Cumulative Bibliography of Bibliographies, 1937- . New York: H. W. Wilson, 1938-

Education Index, Jan. 1929- ; a Cumulative Subject Index to a Selected List of Educational Periodicals, Proceedings and Yearbooks. New York: H. W. Wilson, 1932-

Vertical File Index; Subject and Title Index to Selected Pamphlet Material. New York: H. W. Wilson, 1935-

For free materials see also issues of professional periodicals, such as:

Instructor

Today's Education

Wilson Library Bulletin

Index